INSIGHTS ON
IMPLEMENTATION

IMPROVING FLOW

COLLECTED PRACTICES AND CASES

Productivity Press

New York

Most Productivity Press books are available at quantity discounts when purchased in bulk. For more information contact our Customer Service Department (888-319-5852). Address all other inquiries to:

Productivity Press
444 Park Avenue South, 7th floor
New York, NY 10016
United States of America
Telephone: 212-686-5900
Fax: 212-686-5411
E-mail: info@productivitypress.com

Material originally appeared in the *Lean Manufacturing Advisor*, 2000-2005.

Library of Congress Cataloging-in-Publication Data

Insights on implementation–improved flow : collected practices and cases.
    p. cm.
  "Material originally appeared in the Lean Manufacturing Advisor, 2000-2005."
  Includes bibliographical references and index.
  ISBN 1-56327-332-2 (alk. paper)
  1. Business logistics—Case studies. 2. Industrial management—Case studies.
3. Industrial efficiency—Case studies. I. Productivity Press. II. Lean manufacturing advisor.
  HD38.5.I56 2006
  658.5'03–dc22

                                                                2005034725

08 07 06 05 9 8 7 6 5 4 3 2 1

Contents

Introduction

Flow is a fundamental concept of lean manufacturing. Many of the lean tools are designed to help improve or smooth the flow of parts and materials through your production processes. What these tools can do, when they should be used and how they can be of most value is the focus of this book.

The chapters that follow were originally published as articles in the Lean Manufacturing Advisor newsletter. This compilation is not designed to provide you with instructions on how to use each tool. Rather, these case studies and columns will help you understand the applications of these tools, their benefits and ways to use them to greatest advantage.

Cell design is critical to continuous flow. But while the traditional U-shaped cell is a staple of lean manufacturing, there are numerous techniques for configuring and staffing cells. The chapters in the first section of this book describe the varied approaches to setting up cells taken by several different companies, and also discuss 3P, a lean tool that can help you redesign a cell from scratch.

Finding ways to increase throughput once flow is established is an ongoing effort for a lean company. In the second section, the

---

[1] For more information regarding the articles in this book, including the original dates of publication, please refer to the citations section.

importance of takt time in setting the pace is reviewed, as are other strategies for improving flow – including scrap reduction, building in proper sequence, creating a flexible manufacturing system and eliminating variability.

Smoothing or leveling production flow is the focus of the third section. The chapters here describe the line-balancing tool known as heijunka, some unconventional ways of improving flow through workers who move and workstations that are not stationary, and an unusual approach to scheduling in which employees work 12-hour shifts.

The final section focuses on SMED – single minute exchange of die, a tool for reducing machine changeover time. You will read in these chapters about the key techniques of SMED, ways to calculate changeover costs, a method for properly sequencing changeovers, and the importance of low-tech simulations.

With the knowledge and insights you gain from this material, we hope that your can strengthen your use of these tools, increasing flow through your processes to ever-increasing levels.

Ralph Bernstein
Editor
Lean Manufacturing Advisor

IMPROVING FLOW

COLLECTED PRACTICES AND CASES

Part I

Setting Up Cells

OVERVIEW

Creating a manufacturing cell sounds simple: Put your processes in order, one following another, in a U-shaped configuration. But getting that cell to work smoothly requires a finally tuned design and carefully planned staffing.

Chapter 1 describes how Delphi found that right-sizing equipment was a critical part of proper cell design. Read also how the company designed the cell for flexible staffing and to operate according to a "natural" takt time.

Vulcan Electric is a company that had to adopt a new mind-set when redesigning its cells. Chapter 2 explains how managers had to learn that it was better to fully staff one cell at a time rather than spread staff thinly among all cells.

Creating cells in a job shop, where volume of any given product is too low to justify a dedicated cell, is always a challenge. In chapter 3, learn how Advance Turning and Manufacturing met that challenge by identifying families of parts and by reducing the numbers of tools and raw materials required.

People often think that once a cell is created, its configuration is rarely changed. But at Candela Corporation, cells are often broken down and reconfigured; workstations on wheels are taken by operators from one cell to another. Read about it in Chapter 4.

Sometimes a cell may have been around so long that radical change is necessary to improve performance. That's where the tool known as 3P comes in. Chapter 5 explains 3P and how it was put to use by Freudenberg NOK.

And Chapter 6 describes a different use of 3P – to design the work cell for a new company, Apollo Hardwoods. The firm was able to dramatically cut startup costs and design operations for a targeted capacity by employing 3P.

1

De-Coupling and Coupling: Keys to Better Cell Design

July 2004

When designing a work cell, right-size your equipment, strive for flexibility, and don't base your design on takt time.

By following those simple principles when redesigning a cell in its Flint, Mich., plant, Delphi virtually doubled the cell's output, gained flexibility and improved quality.

One of the key concepts in Delphi's approach was what it calls "de-couple/couple," according to Jeffrey Miller, an operations manager and a manager of the Delphi Manufacturing System.

Delphi realized that a large, highly sophisticated machine used in the cell was, in fact, a constraint — designed for only one product and highly inflexible. Delphi "de-coupled" several functions performed by the machine, replacing it with several smaller machines, each performing only one of the tasks. The company then "coupled" together several different products, all of which could go through smaller machines.

In Search of Flexibility

The cell manufactured electronic instrument clusters for automobiles. These contain indicators and gauges on the dashboard — the speedometer, the fuel gauge, and so on. The clusters were made with a large machine called a staker, which attaches the indicators on to a metal spindle. The cell made from 350 to 400 pieces per day.

Each staker was designed to produce only one product. A different product required a different staker.

Another problem arose from the pace of the work and the capabilities of the machines. Calculations based on customer demand determined that 2.5 stakers were required, meaning three assembly cells. Total takt time per cell — the amount of time available to produce a product, based on demand — was determined to be 70.8 seconds.

"It's very difficult to train people to be able to be repetitive (with a takt time that long)," Miller comments.

In addition, the stakers had little flexibility to respond to changes in demand. Volumes would have to fluctuate by 350 pieces per day to fully utilize one additional shift. And if demand increased by 20 percent, an additional staker would have to be purchased at a cost of $250,000.

"We looked to the future, and we said 'we're not going to be able to get the balance we want with these machines,'" Miller recalls. So "we broke it apart."

The company determined that a staker actually performed four functions: adhering an appliqué, staking the indicators on the spindle, calibration and inspection. Separate pieces of equipment were purchased to perform separate functions.

Then executives reconfigured the equipment to create a "mixed" cell — capable of handling more than one product (see sidebar, p.5). Flexible fixturing was used so that one machine could be used on different products.

Improved Output and Quality

By breaking up the functions of the staker, Delphi achieved what Miller calls a "natural takt time" of about 25 seconds, meaning that is about how long each step in the process now takes. Production is now

How to Redesign a Cell

Before revising its design of a cell staking automotive gauges on a metal spindle, Delphi had separate operations for two products, shown in these diagrams as W and Y, and was anticipating a need to produce a third product, Z.

In the first diagram, the smaller boxes at the bottom represent the first step in the process, that of attaching an appliqué. The middle boxes represent the machine known as a staker attaching and calibrating the gauges, with the top boxes representing inspection.

The process was broken up into smaller pieces, with a new piece of equipment — what is essentially a small press — being used to attach the appliqué, and a new piece of equipment being used at the end for inspection. Staking and calibration occurred together in one piece of equipment (the larger boxes). Breaking things up this way, and adding a line for product Z, increased productivity 24 percent (second diagram).

De-couple

Product W — 3 Shifts
Product Y — 2 Shifts
Product Z — 2 Shifts

The Next Step ...Couple
24% Productivity

Product W — 2 Shifts
Product Y — 2 Shifts
P   Z roc — 2 Shifts

The Goal

"Mixed Cell Concept"

However, with flexible fixturing, workers were able to eliminate several of the presses, so that one set of presses could be used to attach appliqués for all three products. Similarly, one of the inspection machines at the end was eliminated. Also, the stakers in the middle of the process were rearranged so that one operator had access to three stakers rather than two (third diagram). This new cell configuration virtually doubled production over what it had been before any changes.

5

based on a level schedule of the various products being made, but parts flowing to the cell for final assembly are brought in through a pull system. The company still pays attention to takt time, to make sure production satisfies demand, but it was not the basis for designing the cell.

The new cell has flexibility. Manpower can be added or reduced, and volume can be raised or lowered as necessary.

Capacity is now about 800 units per shift. And according to Miller, quality has improved substantially. He attributes this to less variation in the process because it is now easier for operators to learn and repeat all steps in the process.

"This isn't an approach we use just at our facility," Miller notes. "We use it in other areas and other applications. The same concepts and tools apply."

TAKEAWAYS

- Shorter process steps are preferable.
- Right-size your equipment.
- Takt time is not a basis for cell design.

2

Cell Staffing Options (by Vulcan Electric)

Anthony Perna
March 2001

Over the past ten years, I have been involved in three work cell implementations at three different companies. The transition to continuous flow cells from traditional departments where people perform the same operations, isolated from operations upstream or downstream, is difficult, at best. An issue that I've learned must be addressed to produce substantial change is how to staff the new cells. Recently, I experimented to see the effects that different staffing plans can have on production.

We combined two cells, each with two people, into one team. This team works in a cell on the daily requirements of one product for four hours. After finishing it, the team moves into a different cell to work on the daily requirements of a different product for the second half of the day. (See Figures 1 and 2, p. 9.) Nothing is released to the second cell until the second half of the day.

At day's end, both product lines have produced the necessary quantities to ship. There is limited WIP, and we have enough people in each cell to get close to one-piece flow. The product is not dependent on any operations upstream or downstream, so there is no queue time outside the cell.

Preliminary Steps

Using a software package from Taylor Enterprise Dynamics, I first designed a discrete simulation model of the two staffing scenarios for a cell before combining the teams. In the first scenario, two people in two cells transferred product in batches for eight hours. In the second, four people worked in each cell for four hours producing according to one-piece flow.

At the end of the day, each scenario had generated approximately the same amount of product. It occurred to me that staffing and people issues would determine the success or failure of the cell. Rearranging workbenches and machines is relatively easy. The human issues are the hardest to overcome, but tend to make all the difference.

We educated cell team members on the positive effects of variability reduction, quality at the source, and cycle time reduction. This gave them an overall perspective about the improvement effort and helped them answer the question, "What's in it for me?" They found that the one-piece-flow model actually saved time and confusion for them because errors were detected immediately, resulting in less rework, work-in-process (WIP) and clutter in the work cell.

We had to make sure we had the proper staffing level to keep the product flowing to leverage the new cell arrangement. If we just moved equipment around and called it a work cell, but did things the same old way, we wouldn't have made fundamental improvement. The outcome would have been a system that had the same inefficiencies as before. We had to fundamentally change the way people moved product through each operation.

I've seen so-called cells in which an operator walks the product through each operation, processing the full batch at each station. The cell produces some benefit from having equipment closer because part and people travel distances are shorter.

But such cells don't make any significant gains in reducing WIP, scrap, rework, throughput, and cycle time. Such improvements require uninterrupted flow, which is difficult to achieve in traditional batch manufacturing.

8

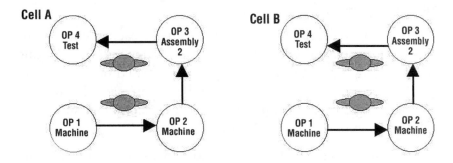

Figure 1. In this conventional scenario, two operators staff each cell for eight hours.

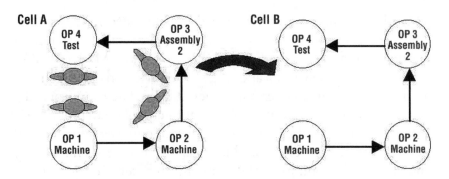

Figure 2. A more radical but effective staffing solution was to staff one cell for half a day, then move the entire team to the other cell.

In conventional manufacturing, a job is started and gets partially down the line. Then it hits a parts shortage and is put aside. A new job is started until it, too, hits a shortage. Everyone stays busy, but little product gets all the way through the system. No revenues are generated because nothing is ready to ship. You use resources and raw material that must be reordered.

Many so-called "cells" are minimally staffed with just enough people to get work out during eight hours. This sounds reasonable from a traditional point of view. Everyone is busy working.

But if the proper staffing is established based on balancing the line, then the product is handed off one piece at a time, or as close to it as practical, thus minimizing cycle time and WIP.

Balancing Work

We started by mapping the value stream for each product, conducting time observations of operators in each of the two cells, and determining the takt time for each product based on its sales history. Once we knew the average number of units needed per day to meet customer demand, we combined machining, subassembly, and assembly operations into a cell.

This gave us data-driven information to model our cell with. Opinions and emotions were kept to a minimum. We balanced each operator's tasks so they filled, but did not exceed, takt time.

One of the main obstacles we faced was the need for cross-training. People in the work cells had to know all of the operations upstream and downstream from their old jobs. Most operators enjoyed having new skills and a less repetitive workday. Each cell is fully staffed with an operator at each station. The team works the necessary amount of hours in one cell to complete that day's output requirements. Then, as a team, everyone moves into a second cell to work on a different product line. The team goes in, finishes the job, and gets out. Jobs release and finish faster. Our production mix changes from day to day, so the time spent in each cell will vary, but the amount of people remains constant.

More Product Shipped

This is contrary to how most supervisors staff their departments. They take a constant or fixed time, say eight hours, and vary the amount of people in each cell by the workload. Instead of having two or three people in each of three work cells producing parts, we have a team spending partial days in each work cell, completing the pieces in less time from start to finish.

With a varying customer demand, everyone had to get used to staying together as a team. In all honesty, there are still times when the shop floor resorts to "old ways." Usually we make a conscious decision to do so and try to minimize this backsliding.

Operators work alongside their counterparts upstream and downstream right in the cell. This smoothes out production by acting as a natural brake on the tendency to over-produce or under-produce. At any given time throughout the day, we have less WIP, quicker defect detection, less rework, better throughput, simpler scheduling, and less variability.

Typically, it is hard for supervisors faced with lots of orders, not to put a couple of people in each cell. Ignoring some products for any period of time to fully complete one product line's demand is not something they are comfortable with. They want to have every cell going. Unfortunately, they have a lot of work being performed with very little shippable product until the end of the day.

By doing each cell's daily workload one by one, we get product to the shipping department much earlier in the day. We are fortunate in having parts that are relatively small so we can store raw materials at point-of-use in the cells.

The majority of our product lines are low-volume and custom-made but the operations are repetitive. Job orders are in the range of 10 to 50 pieces. This is ideal for small lot production. *As we are all quickly learning, variability is the archenemy of a waste-free environment.* Time and variability go hand in hand. The longer a job is open in the system, the more variability it will introduce.

Results

Our goal when we started was to increase the number of job order turns. Since then, we have taken WIP from over $200,000 to under $75,000 on a consistent basis. This is a 62 percent reduction.

We still produce the same amount of product per day as before. But, because we are closer to one-piece flow, we use less resources due to reductions in scrap, rework, travel, transportation, and breaking into partially completed jobs.

Companies trying to create lean work cells must address staffing issues. In dealing with this tough issue, we used tools such as percent loading charts, line leveling, operation consolidation and elimination, constraint pacing, and takt time calculations to arrive at the correct staffing level.

Most importantly, we scheduled time to train, train, and train to instill a value creation mentality in which shippable product is the goal, not just keeping people busy and working hard.

Staffing work cells appropriately smoothes out much of the other activities in the plant and generates the full benefits of cellular manufacturing. Work began to fly through our factory. Inventory levels came down substantially, and cash flow became smoother and more evenly distributed throughout the month because products leave the plant at a more constant rate from day to day.

Anthony Perna now is vice president at an electrical heating manufacturer near Portland, Maine. With a background in engineering and manufacturing, he has worked for a number of companies implementing lean manufacturing.

TAKEAWAYS

- Fully staffing one cell at a time may be more efficient than spreading staff thinly among several cells.
- Such a plan will face resistance from supervisors who do not like to see cells idle.
- Cross-training is essential for the plan to succeed.

3

Job Shop Breaks Traditional Rules with 1 -Piece Flow Cells

December 2001

As a successful job shop, Advance Turning and Manufacturing, Inc. makes a wide variety of metal and plastic precision parts, primarily for the aerospace and medical industries. Products include couplings and fittings for airplane fuel and hydraulic lines, components for powered surgical instruments, prosthetic devices, and components used in peritoneal kidney dialysis, as well as some firearm parts. Primary processes are CNC turning and milling.

Founded in 1972, the privately owned Jackson, Mich., company has grown steadily. It now has sales of approximately 10 million and employs 64 full-time people. Despite its track record of profitability, the unsettled economic climate of the early 1990s concerned company founder and CEO John Macchia, Sr. Close to home, the auto and aerospace industries were sluggish. In Washington, D.C., the Clinton Administration's sweeping proposals for the health care industry were creating uncertainty about how the industry's cost structure would be affected.

"Everybody was nervous about what was going to happen, so they started to focus on costs and driving prices down in the early '90s," recalled Macchia's son John, who is Advance's president. "There was no more passing the costs on to the customer," he said.

Customers were saying, 'This is what I can afford for this part. You find a way to make it at that price.' And it wasn't just our customers," said Macchia. "It was our customers' customers and their customers."

Also driving the company to lean was the desire to gain greater control of the whipsawing job shop environment where a customer averaging $225,000 in orders per month can suddenly go to $325,000 for a month. "The only way we could take control was making what the customer needed, when the customer needed it, and only what they needed," said Macchia. Because job shop parts are unique to each customer, it's risky to rely on inventory as a buffer.

"If we make excess inventory for one of our customers and they decide they don't want the part anymore, there's nobody else we can sell it to in the world," said Macchia. "It's scrap. Customers can change a product, delete a product, or revise a product, and we're stuck with what we have." That is a strong incentive to reduce inventory and shorten lead times so you can make parts when the customer's order is firm.

With economic conditions heralding the need for better efficiency and control, the only question for the company about implementing lean was, "Do we get on the bandwagon now, or wait," said Macchia.

Reforming the Company

The answer came when Macchia, Sr., attended a workshop on implementing lean at the invitation of Aeroquip, a nearby customer in Jackson that was pursuing a lean conversion of its own. About halfway through the program, the senior Macchia "got it," recalled his son. The instructors started talking about one-piece flow "and that's when the light came on."

A week later, Macchia, Sr., put the company on the path to a lean conversion. "We shut the company down for an afternoon and took everyone out to a restaurant for snacks and a drink and said we were reforming the company," Macchia recalled.

There was no crisis. The company was doing well. So management held the meeting outside the shop to demonstrate the gravity of the situation. Part of the message to people was that Advance had to change if it wanted to remain successful. Managers told people the company was "going to be the leader" in implementing lean in its industry. "We are going to be the first, and you guys will have good jobs with good benefits," Macchia said. "We are profitable today, but in five years if we don't do these things, we will not be profitable, we will not be growing. If we want to be in business in 30 years, and you want to retire out of this company, we need to do this."

Company officials set up a flip chart on an easel. They drew a big circle on it and labeled it the "new Advance Turning." They drew lines running into the circle and labeled them with a lot of new terms like kanban, cells, and lean. In explaining the terms and the role of each in lean production, they also predicted to the 20-plus employees who worked at Advance at the time, "Some of you will leave. You will not want to do this."

The other part of the message was that the changes would start right away. A couple of weeks later, the company parked rented dumpsters near the building and began filling them with unneeded items and old parts from the shop. "What's really scary is that it seemed at the time like such a radical change," said Chuck Parylak, vice president of manufacturing.

The housekeeping effort prepared the company to create its first cell with help from an Aeroquip engineer and a state grant to cover some of the cost of the initial training. Still, building the first cell was largely a trial-and-error process, recalled Parylak.

Finding Families

'The first thing we looked at was what do we want this cell to make?" he said. To make the effort on the first cell worthwhile, they wanted to dedicate enough volume to it to support work on two or three shifts. "We just wanted to start off with something that gave us a chance to succeed," said Parylak. In a small job shop, a cell running production only on one shift probably wouldn't profitably cover the cost of the equipment in it.

To determine what parts to run in the cell, the cell design team identified a "family" of parts that shared a similar processing sequence. The team didn't create a product family matrix. To determine what parts belong in a family, a cross-functional cell design team asked the question, What kind of parts can we make without changing any tools at all?

The parts didn't have to look exactly alike. The key was not having to change the tooling on the CNC turret to make them. "We weren't going to pull the tools off the turret anymore. We were going to use the same tools on every job even if we had to rewrite every program — which we had to do," said Parylak.

Operator input was valuable during what were called "zero-setup meetings" during the cell's design. "Basically, we tried to tool up the machines, so we changed the least amount of tools possible going from one part number to the next," Parylak explained. Eventually, Advance went from using more than 200 tools plantwide, to 70 or 80 today.

Standardized Programming

There was another incentive for rewriting the CNC programs besides the desire to avoid changing tools. In creating part families, Advance discovered some parts did not fit in any cell. At that point, the company studied the leftover parts to determine if they could be made in a different way so they could fit into a family. Often, different people just had different CNC programming styles. The results were similar parts made with different tools. By standardizing the way it programmed to make certain types of parts, Advance discovered that many leftover parts could fit into families made with the same tools. "You can make a family by changing your programming style," Macchia advised.

But the acid test of cell was the shop floor. "There's just a lot of trial and error," said Macchia. "You've got to build the first cell,

16

understand it, get it going, then move forward. I don't think you want to try to create six cells in one week. You want to do one, and understand it before moving forward."

"One thing we learned from Aeroquip was that if the cell isn't right the first time, just keep trying until it's right," said Parylak. The team changed the layout, part mix, and staffing level "probably five or six times" before it was satisfied with the first cell. For example, when machines were first moved into a cell "it didn't do any good because it still took the same amount of time to set up the machines," Parylak recalled. That led to standardizing tooling in the cell turret. "Slowly you add all the pieces to the puzzle," he said.

Leaders Emerge

The first cell had two and three people operating three machines arranged in a straight line according to processing sequence. Equipment was ultimately rearranged in a U-shape to minimize operator walking distances and permit staffing by one operator. Initially, operators didn't think one person could run three machines at once and still produce a quality product.

"Some people don't like change, recalled Macchia. "We lost several people who just didn't want to come along. Others jumped at the chance. Then you had a big group in the middle that had to be convinced one way or the other. Once we built the first cell, a lot of people jumped on the bandwagon, and then we couldn't rearrange the rest of the machines fast enough. We had planned on doing one or two cells a year, and we had the whole shop done in six months because everybody wanted to do it."

"Fortunately, we've got a great group of people," said Parylak. After all is said and done, it all boils down to the operator. He or she is where the new cell succeeds or fails."

Another factor in the company's ultimate success is that "everybody wears a lot of hats." People are willing to pitch in to do what needs to be done. For instance, the maintenance manager not only does maintenance, but also is a journeyman machinist, an electrician, and a plumber. "It's like that with a lot of our operators and support people. That has really been a big help."

Another big help was seeing the owner, John Macchia, Sr., on the floor helping people and learning with them. "When the guy who signs your paycheck is out there cheering everybody on, it helps a lot," said Parylak. "It is a long process, and you really do have to have commitment," he said.

Aeroquip was helpful, too. When Advance ran into a problem, it could talk to an Aeroquip engineer about what to do.

Leaders emerged from among employees as the nascent lean cell developed. These "high-energy and self-motivated" people were among the first to work in the new cell, said company officials. In the lunchroom, they talked about how much better working in the cell was compared to the old way of tending one machine. They also helped explain what was being done and why.

For instance, setup is a waste to be minimized or eliminated in a lean conversion. But in the traditional job shop, an operator usually runs one machine. They spend hours setting it up for the next operation, and they enjoy it because setup is different. It introduces some variety.

What operators didn't realize at first is that cell work contains a lot of variety. They give up long setups, but they order their own material through a pull system, maintain their own inventory and tooling, and no longer have the frustration of searching the shop for gauging and tooling because it is dedicated to the cell. "Our people are challenged all day long," said Macchia. Each cell functions, in effect, as the operator's own self-sufficient machine shop.

They also share responsibility for running the cell schedule with management. Parylak equipped cells with PCs to help operators manage them. They don't have to phone engineering for a program to be sent out to a machine. Programs reside on the cell's PC.

The PC screens give operators the schedule of what to make, but they can suggest changes, for example, if they see a better way to minimize changes of tooling or raw material. Jobs are scheduled in due-date order and by part family. The scheduling program, which Parylak developed in-house, puts a variety of information a click away from operators, including the number of parts to make, SPC charts, when to change tooling, the order due date, the number of hours anticipated for the job, anticipated setup time, how many parts have been made, if the operator is ahead or behind, if the cell will have to work overtime, if the raw material is in, if the CNC program is ready, and if there is a blueprint in the shop for the part. A field for comments allows operators in the same cell but on different shifts to communicate.

Three Types of Cells

Communication was an important part of the overall effort. As the company created more cells, more people got the chance to work on a cell design team. And operators were free to walk over and observe a cell's operation. Such opportunities helped spread an understanding of lean concepts.

The actual cell design resembled a kaizen event, but less formal. "We didn't have time or money for that; we had to make parts," explained Macchia. On a weekend, people would scrape floors clean, then brainstorm in a conference room about creating the cell, walk back to the shop and move the machines, brainstorm again in a conference room for a few minutes about where to position inventory or finished goods, then walk back to the shop and implement the ideas.

During the next few days, the person championing the cell along with the cell design team members would, in effect, do the follow-up, making sure that CNC programs were rewritten, and that actions to standardize tooling, gauging, and raw materials were carried out. Over six months, the departments of like-machines — milling, lathe, debur, etc., were broken up into cells.

Although some cells are dedicated to a part family from a particular customer, there also are cells that run families consisting of parts

19

from different customers. This is done to get adequate volume in the cell. Some cells have broader job mixes than others. Advance part families can include many different products and customers. One cell runs 400 different part numbers, but there are similarities in the tooling used to make the parts.

In contrast, a cell for a pharmaceutical customer never changes. It's one machine only runs one part number and is operated only when the customer wants parts. "But there are not too many job shops that can afford to let equipment sit on the floor like that and make any money," Macchia said.

Basically, the 20 cells in the 30, 000 square-foot shop fall into one of three categories:

1. Zero-setup cells — Tooling in turrets are fixed allowing setups to be reduced to a range of 25 to 30 minutes for all three machines. Fifteen minutes or less is the goal. About half the cells fall into this category, which is the most advanced in implementing lean concepts.

2. Long- run cells — Setups require four to eight hours to do all three machines or longer if the job is very difficult. These generally handle a couple of parts with longer runs.

3. Odds & ends — These run the parts that don't fit into any of the first two cells. These are the toughest cells for implementing lean concepts.

One-Piece Flow

The goal of cellular production was one-piece flow. One-piece flow forced the company to wean itself from wasteful batch-and-queue practices that haunt many job shops. For instance, in a 100-piece order, the first department might run 110 because they knew some would be lost along the way either during setups or to quality problems, explained Frank Lusebrink, Jr., vice president and chief financial officer.

When the batch got to the next processing department, the production schedule might be a little off, so the parts would sit in containers, waiting to be processed. This batch-and-queue, stop-and-start journey would probably happen through the subsequent processing departments, too. Finally, the order would be ready to ship. "And we'd either have 98 or 102," said Lusebrink.

Now, the company had to store the extra two or rush to make up the missing two. If the order were two parts short, production of the missing parts would jump ahead of others in the batch-and-queue procession, thus making the schedule just a little more off for the next order.

If the order was two over, the extra ones would be stored in an inventory room, guaranteeing that when the customer placed the same order in a few months, the parts could not be found or had been forgotten. Naturally, they'd be rediscovered during the annual discarding of inventory that couldn't be sold.

In contrast, making parts one at a time in processing sequence requires the cell operator to unload a part from the first CNC machine, which then advances the bar stock and begins making the next piece. The operator walks the part from the first machine to the second machine, arriving as the second machine finishes processing its part. The operator unloads the piece in the second machine and loads the piece from the first one. At the third machine, the operator unloads the piece as processing ends and loads the part just removed from the second machine. The piece removed from the final machine is done, except perhaps for a quality check or deburring. Cells have quality gauges and small debur units placed in sequence.

"Any problem along the way is caught right away," said Parylak. "The operator is in control from the start of the job to the end of the job."

Macchia estimated that most jobs go from raw material to invoice in one day. He noted that the average invoice size is about $450, so the company doesn't have the benefit of many long part runs or of making "Gucci" parts.

Standardization

The one-piece-flow choreography can't happen without standardization. Standardizing programming routines helped create part families. Now, Advance applied the concept to other areas. Machining methods and tooling in machine turrets were standardized based on part families running across the cells. "You're saying that anytime you see a particular shape, this is the tool you're going to use," said Parylak."This is how you're going to attack the part. You do that the same way in every cell."

Instead of using 10 different types of bar stocks, "we use three" to make all parts, noted Parylak. Using stock that is a little too big might mean adding a penny or two to a part, but saving the time and cost of repeatedly changing collets, tools, and bar stock sizes more than makes up for the pennies. Drill sizes are standardized. Instead of stocking a variety of sizes, cells stock only the specific drills or tools that are needed in the cell. Operators drill down to the nearest quarter inch and bore out the rest of the material.

The big benefit of standardizing turrets and machining methods was elimination or dramatic reductions of setup times. Standardizing bar stock and storing it at the point of use along with the tooling needed in a cell added to the progress in cutting lead times and costs. "Operators don't have to run across the shop to get bar stock because it's right here next to the cell," explained Parylak. "They don't have to run across to the tool crib because it's right here in the cabinet. You're constantly saving time."

Kanban Replenishment

Raw material is replenished through a combination kanban/fax system that Advance began implementing in 1998. When consumption of stock reaches a trigger point, the cell operator removes a small plastic kanban card from the bundle of stock and slips it into a collection envelope hanging in the cell. The tool crib supervisor walks a route every morning to collect the kanban cards. Back at the crib, he or she uses a scanner to read a bar code on each card. Then the supervisor returns the cards to an "ordered" envelope hanging in the cell.

The scanned information is transmitted by phone to the supplier, where it generates a fax print-out. The bar code tells the supplier the raw material needed, the quantity needed, and identifies the consuming cell. Advance uses one supplier for virtually everything from bar stock to rest room supplies. Whatever items the main vendor doesn't carry, it procures by a requisition order faxed to a secondary supplier.

Raw material arrives at the receiving dock with a label identifying the destination cell. A material handler takes the material directly to the cell where it is stored on a small rack near the first machine. All of the zero-setup cells are on the replenishment system, and others are implementing it.

The system assures that operators, instead of retrieving raw material, spend more time adding value to parts, which is what the cus-

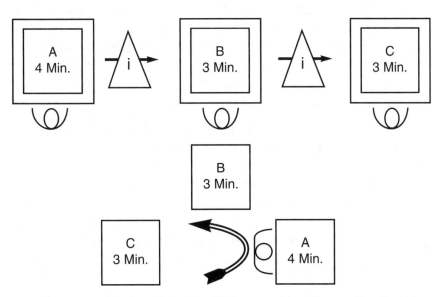

The diagram shows a batch production line with three operators at three machines in widely separated departments. Parts sit idle in inventory in between processes. At best, lead time would be 10 minutes. In the bottom diagram, an operator moves the parts in one-piece flow. After the first part, lead time is 4 minutes.

tomer is paying for, which is how the company makes money, explained Macchia. "The most important customer besides the external customer is the machine operator. They've got to be making parts."

In a lean system versus a traditional system, operators make more parts, faster and cheaper. For instance, imagine a traditional production system with three machines, A, B, and C. The cycle times are four minutes, three minutes, and three minutes, respectively. With an operator staffing each machine, it takes 10 minutes and three operators to get a part, explained Macchia.

If the same machines are arranged in a cell with one operator moving the parts to each machine to keep the parts moving in a continuous flow, "every four minutes you're getting a part after the first part," Macchia said. "You have four minutes and one operator. The benefit is pretty obvious. That's how we looked at it."

While noting that every job shop is different, Macchia, Parylak, and Lusebrink distilled out of the Advance experience some key actions and concepts that applied in their case. They may help you fashion lean production cells in a job shop, or a job shop area within a repetitive facility. The steps are listed in a rough order of use, but keep in mind that, as in most lean implementations, the tools must be applied more or less simultaneously.

Group parts into families. Manufacturers in high-variety environments often reject lean production, thinking it can't handle the diversity. "Find the commonality in the diversity," advised Lusebrink. You may think you have diversity that is unmanageable in a lean system "but you really don't when you look at it," he said. Examine your parts, asking, "What tools does it take to make this part," he said. Parts might be different shapes but require the same tools. Some cells don't have any parts that look alike, but use the same tool.

Arrange equipment in processing sequence. On the shop floor, the first action you want to take is the most important — create flow

by arranging equipment so parts move through the cell in processing sequence. Advance made sure each cell had all the right equipment needed to produce a finished product, including gauging and
debur stations. The only operation that occurs outside the cell is
washing before shipment.

Configure equipment so the operator has the shortest walking distance, which usually is a U-shape. "You don't want a big broad cell
where the operator has to walk half a mile back and forth to get
parts," said Parylak.

To determine the cell's production rate, go with the "benchmark
machine," said Macchia. This is the slowest machine, which sets
the pace for the cell. This constraint becomes the focus for
improvement efforts to reduce cycle time.

Most cells at Advance have three machines. The CNC mill usually
is the slowest. If the mill has a five-minute cycle time and the two
lathes in the cell each have two-minute cycle times, "we don't even
worry about the lathes," said Macchia. Let the lathes idle for three
minutes during processing while you work on reducing the mill's
cycle time. "The slowest machine is the cost driver, and the other
two machines are running for free," said Macchia.

This is a tough concept for many job shop owners who become
anxious at the sight of a spindle not turning and making parts. It can
adversely affect their efforts at lean cellular production. "If they
have a job in a cell with three machines and a job required only two
machines in the cell, they still would try to run other parts into the
cell to utilize the third machine."

The result is confusion for the scheduler and for operators who must
try to run two processes in their workspace at the same time, said
Lusebrink. Letting a machine sit idle is actually more efficient in a
lean shop. The higher machine utilization gained from lean techniques such as setup time reduction, one-piece flow, and standardization, far outweighs occasionally not using a machine in a cell. In
fact, Advance's machine utilization is better than when machines

25

were grouped in departments. Moving batches of parts from department to department resulted in long changeovers and hidden quality problems that ultimately drained machine utilization.

Remember that high machine efficiency doesn't equal lower costs. The biggest gain comes from producing exactly what the customer is paying for, in the exact amount, exactly when wanted. Making parts in one-piece flow creates the lowest total costs by minimizing the amount of material and time at all stages of production.

Lusebrink noted that there are ways to balance out the flow in a cell where machines have different cycle times. For instance, you can go halfway through a part instead of all the way, then put the rest of the drilling or boring on another machine. Shortening the first machine's cycle time and lengthening the second one's allows you to run both in a constant flow.

Standardize tooling and programs. Pulling together a family of parts won't automatically reduce the cell's tooling because people program jobs in different ways with different tools. Parts can look very similar but have very different cycle times. You could find yourself with a cell that produces little benefit because it requires a lot of lengthy changeovers between parts.

Advance discovered that moving machines into cells required it to standardize machine tooling and programming, noted Parylak. Standardizing the tooling in the turret forced the company to standardize the programming. A cell design team included a "program champion" who led the effort to standardize tooling and reduce it, he said.

Champions asked questions like, "What can we use to bore that will cut every bore that needs to be done?" he said. The champion's responsibility was to ensure development of parts programs so common features in a family were programmed the same way. Reprogramming was a "three to four month" process per cell, but "you immediately see results," said Parylak, as scrap falls and throughput increases.

Advance also standardizes equipment, buying most of it from the same manufacturer. This makes training easier and consistent. It also allows jobs to be set up the same way, with the same tools on all shifts. A single machine setup took several hours in batch production. Now, an entire cell can be set up in an average of one or two hours depending on the job.

Develop support for the cell. Locate bar stock and tooling at the point of use — at the cell — to eliminate waiting. Establish a pull system for replenishment.

Close to Quitting

One step that Advance didn't take was an extensive planning and cost analysis of the benefits of switching to lean. "In hindsight, maybe we would have seen that the first year would be terrible," said Lusebrink. "But maybe it would have kept us from even starting."

The first year of the lean transition cost dearly. The company nearly called off the effort. "We were a very profitable company in 1991," Macchia recalled. In 1992, the lean effort began. A year later, Advance was profitable, but less so. The drop was due to the time spent training people and gaining experience in getting the flow right in the cells.

"It just took some time to get going," Macchia recalled. At 18 months, "we really hit bottom and we came closest to saying, 'Let's just line the machines up like we used to do and go back.' But we knew this was the right thing to do and we could see the fruits of our labor starting to come around."

"Once we got through that," recalled Parylak, "pretty soon everybody was getting really good at it, and new ideas started coming in from operators and support people. Pretty soon you can't even fathom going back to the old ways."

Financial results in 93 topped 91. "Every year we've been able to reduce costs to our customers and either maintain or increase profitability," noted Macchia. Lean has cut labor costs in half as a percent of sales, but doubled employment to more than 60 people. The increased capacity garnered from the improvements has let Advance bid on — and win — more work. The company has moved into a new facility, which includes a workout area for employees in a loft where inventory would have been stored.

With traditional job shop methods, company officials noted, producing the volume of work the company now handles would require a much larger staff with more supervisors, schedulers, material handlers, and a stock room staff.

"It's easy to give up along the way because it's totally going to change the way you do business," said Parylak. Without commitment at the top, management will probably back away from the time and expense in moving equipment, cleaning, and training. "Getting through that time is the most difficult period. You'll see a point where you want to give up because we saw it too," he said. "All the improvements you make along the way do have a cost. You will reap rewards; it's just a matter of time. Once you start to see the returns, they'll just boggle your mind."

TAKEAWAYS

- To implement cells in a job shop, reduce the number of tools required by rewriting CNC programs, and reduce the different types of raw material.
- Improve the cell through trial and error; don't expect it to be right the first time.
- Profits may drop in the first year due to time spent training and gaining experience.

4

Cells on Wheels Give Company Ability to Shift Course Quickly

December 2004

If you want your manufacturing cells to be as flexible as possible, make sure everything in the cells is on wheels. Candela Corporation has done that, which enables the company to respond rapidly when demand changes and when new products are introduced.

Cells can be set up and broken down easily. Workers take mobile workstations with them when they move from one cell to another.

"We can clear an area and have it empty, prepare point-of-use inventory on carts, roll it in and be up and running in a short period of time," says Mike Duquette, director of materials at the Wayland, Mass., maker of medical lasers. "The whole idea of the cell is to be flexible."

Part of that flexibility is that every worker in final assembly has his or her own mobile workstation. There are only six of these workers (Duquette notes that the 150-employee company is "engineering heavy"), and they move among six manufacturing cells. A cell involves one to three workstations, and at any given time, fluctuations in demand may dictate that some cells are busy while others sit idle.

The employee who uses this mobile station in a manufacturing cell at Candela Corporation takes it with him when he moves to a different cell, typically once or twice a week.

"There is some common stuff across all the cells," Duquette explains. "That is what we are putting into the mobile workstations. When an operator goes to any of the cells, it is easy for them to take that with them."

Specifically, the workstation includes the operator's tools, certain documentation and some free stock — bolts, o-rings and the like.

"The alternative would be that the tools specific to that cell, the free stock, would already be there," he adds. "Since it's used across all the different cells, it's easier for us to put it in a mobile workstation. Not to mention that people like to have an ownership for their things, their tools."

The flexibility of the new arrangement is already producing benefits for Candela, Duquette contends, even though the cells were only put in place in July 2004, about six months ago. On-time delivery has improved, inventory is down and consolidation of the supply base (a related aspect of the lean transformation) has brought down the cost of materials.

Going Mobile

The medical lasers made by Candela are used for elimination of birthmarks, treatment of tattoos, scars, and warts, and hair removal. Duquette, who had previously been a lean consultant, joined the company at a time when Candela had begun only minimal efforts to become lean.

As he began efforts to transform the company, Duquette noticed that each assembly worker had his or her own desk on the shop floor. The desks were rarely used, but contained the free stock the workers needed. Duquette eliminated the desks, but they became his inspiration for the mobile workstations. The workstations are off-the-shelf products, each costing about $1,000.

The desks were one part of what Duquette says was a "very fragmented" operation: "It was departmentalized, not product-oriented, a lot of work in process. The operator basically walked around the plant picking out parts." Noting that lean improvement efforts often involve making so-called "spaghetti diagrams" to track worker movements, Duquette comments, "ours was a gigantic bowl of spaghetti."

Butterflies and Bread

Today, things are different. The cells are set up in what Duquette describes as an "eight-winged butterfly" arrangement taking up about 10,000 square feet of space. The movable carts that are used to create the cells are stocked with the necessary parts, and those are replenished through a three-bin kanban system. When the assembly workers need to replenish the small items in their mobile workstations, they go to a central carousel where those items are stored. (The carousel is regularly replenished by a so-called "bread man" program, a comparison to the worker who brings fresh bread in to replenish shelves in a supermarket.)

Workers typically move from one cell to another about once or twice a week, depending on shifts in demand. Introduction of a new product can lead to creation of a new cell — an easy task with everything on wheels. The company tries to introduce one or two new products a year.

Duquette concedes that when he introduced the mobile workstations, "operators didn't like it right away. After a while, when we had been very successful, and they could build products more quickly, more efficiently, and were more flexible, I think the operators liked it better."

To build buy-in, he involved the operators in the process of developing the workstations, initially buying just a couple and asking the operators to approve the choice. "They had a vested interest in what we were doing. If you ask them today, they'll say they want to be more involved with changes."

One operator didn't like the new carts, but "you go with the 80-20 rule," Duquette states. "If the majority are happy, it's probably the right way to go."

But he adds, "the number one problem with any of these changes is dealing with the changes. People do not like change. It tends to get worse before it gets better. You need to persevere through that. Leadership and direction are so important."

Measurable Success

Candela gauges the progress of its lean transformation primarily with three major metrics.

The first is on-time delivery, which Duquette says really wasn't being measured when he started with the company, though employees knew they were frequently late because of parts shortages. Duquette established a baseline, and while he declines to say how bad it was, he does say that the on-time percentage has improved by 50 percent.

Inventory is the second major metric, and Duquette boasts that the value of days-on-hand inventory has dropped from about $8 million to $6.5 million, with $1 million of that decline coming in the first quarter of implementation.

The third metric is purchase price variance (PPV). That relates to the fact that Candela dramatically reduced its supplier base. "We leveraged in on the core suppliers we were spending money with, gave them more business and explained how we want to operate from a cellular manufacturing side," he explains, adding that the remaining suppliers were also told "we don't want to be short, ever" and were told Candela wanted to increase inventory turns.

By giving the suppliers more business — along with longer-term orders — "we were able to show a commitment to them and get a reduced price," Duquette explains. "We've gotten tremendous gains in PPV, and that's reflected in our profitability."

For the quarter ending Oct. 2 of 2004, Candela reported that revenues were up 20 percent to $22.4 million, while earnings jumped from just below $1.8 million to more than $2.8 million.

Duquette remains an unabashed advocate of cells on wheels. "I don't really see it as not being appropriate anywhere," he declares. "You have the ability to move product around quickly. I can't see that as being anything but positive. Anything that is immovable hardware is a deterrent to your ability to change."

TAKEAWAYS

- Putting all stations in a cell on wheels increases flexibility.
- Giving employees mobile workstations builds a sense of ownership.
- Operators should be involved in workstation setup to build buy-in.

5

Time to Take A Radical Step Forward

August 2002

Sometimes a company falls under what James Vatalaro likes to call a "kaizen cloud."

Vatalaro explains that an ongoing kaizen program can reach a point of diminishing returns, or "kaizen burnout," as he also calls it. The improvements gained from repeatedly attacking manufacturing processes with kaizen events may seem to be getting smaller.

That's when it's time for kaikaku, a Japanese term meaning radical change. And one form of kaikaku is the process known as 3P. (See sidebar, p. 40, for a definition.)

In this chart at Freudenberg NOK in Cleveland, Ga., process alternatives for molding – identified by the numbers across the top – are evaluated according to the criteria listed down the left. Alternative number 5 is chosen because it has the highest total score.

While there is some disagreement as to what 3P stands for (see sidebar, page 36), the essence of 3P is to review product design and process design starting with a blank sheet of paper. A 3P effort goes beyond trying to improve an existing product or process; in 3P, Vatalaro says, "altering product design and process design are fair game. Those are traditionally a no-fly zone."

Methods for Evaluating Alternatives

At Freudenberg NOK, two of the most critical steps in a 3P kaizen event are the development and then the evaluation of alternatives for accomplishing a process step. This typically takes place on the second afternoon through the third morning of a five-day 3P event (see diagram of schedule, p. 39).

The overall goal of this development is to come up with creative ways to achieve an identified process step that is consistent with lean principles.

How? First, team members are charged with identifying a minimum of seven different ways that each process step can be accomplished.

For example, if the step is to create a hole in a piece of material, the seven alternatives might be to drill, stamp, cut, punch, burn, blow or mold the hole in place.

Next, the team must identify the method by which each alternative would be accomplished. For example, burning the hole might involve using an acetylene torch.

The team continues by defining the gauge that will be used to assure the process step has been performed. And finally, any tools, fixtures and/or machines that are required must be defined.

Guidelines for developing these alternatives include:
- Use one page for each process step.
- First think about options or alternatives for accomplishing the process step. An alternative for cleaning a part may be not to contaminate it in the first place.
- Avoid thinking about machines until the alternatives and methods have been developed.

Next comes evaluation of the alternatives. To accomplish this process, team members must:
- Determine the appropriate lean criteria to evaluate the alternatives. (In his conference presentation, Gary VanWambeke of the company listed 22 potential criteria, from meeting takt time to SMED changeover to use of familiar technology. Perhaps five of these might be chosen as the criteria for evaluating any partic-

At the Freudenberg NOK plant in Cleveland, Ga., 3P techniques are being used to completely redesign manufacturing

ular set of alternatives.)
- Weight each criterion on a scale of one to ten, based on the relative importance to a lean system.
- List the seven alternative proposals across column headings. The first proposal should have the current process or baseline condition.
- Evaluate how each proposal compares to the baseline. The baseline is five. Better proposals are rated higher, worse lower.
- For each proposal, multiply its rating on a particular criterion by the weight for that criterion. Add the totals for all criteria to calculate the score.
- The best proposal is the one with the highest score.

Next, the team takes the best alternative for each step and puts them together into a plan for a manufacturing cell. In this stage, the best processing methods must be selected for each step considering:
- Degree of jidoka — a term meaning autonomation of machines so that they can automatically detect a defective part — immediately stop themselves to prevent it from moving forward, and ask for help.
- Flow creation, to minimize wasted motions by operators, provide minimal staffing and facilitate operator flexibility. "You might have some things where, when you put them together, they just don't flow," VanWambeke notes.
- Layout, making sure operator stations are narrow and walking distance is minimized.
- Quality assurance, so that quality is ensured before the product is passed on to the next process, in a manner consistent with process capabilities.
- Profit, meaning the examination of the relative profitability of alternative plans at realistic demands, considering competitive market price; total cost, including not just investment costs, but running costs and the cost of sustaining quality; both current and intermediate volume projections; and design of the production system at steps of volume increments.

cells. More broadly, according to Gary VanWambeke, site executive at the plant, Freudenberg NOK sees 3P as a way to assure that quality is built into processes, design products for ease of manufacturing, and design manufacturing processes with built-in error-proofing devices.

VanWambeke described the 3P activities at his plant at the 2002 Shingo Prize conference in Covington, Ky. He stated the mission of 3P as being to guarantee process capability, meet takt time and minimize resources.

In one particular example, he said, a 3P effort redesigned a manufacturing cell so that the floor space it required was cut by two-thirds, from 1,200 square meters to 400.

At its Georgia plant, Freudenberg NOK makes engine and transmission seals. About 450 people work at the 150,000-square-foot facility.

Executives hold what they call 3P kaizen events — five days devoted to redesigning processes, following a very specific schedule (see diagram, page 39). Some of the most important steps of that process involve creating and evaluating alternatives (described above). That creative period is "where the rubber hits the road," Van Wambeke says.

Evaluating alternatives is not just a paper exercise. It leads to creation of a full-scale mock-up of a cell, with team members conducting simulations to make sure they have chosen the best design. Near its end, the event involves redefinitions of such metrics as cycle time and process capability based on the new design.

Process and Product

Vatalaro suggests that the approach to cell design described by Van Wambeke is not a true 3P process.

"A risk exists to confuse a 3P project with a kaizen type of event, and there's a world of difference between the two," he says. In a true 3P event, he says, "while you're working on product design, in parallel you're working on process design. The product design is not firm."

3P Kaizen Schedule

	Monday	Tuesday	Wednesday	Thursday	Fri
A M		Information Phase • Kaizen Objectives • Part Numbers • Volume Ramp Up • Takt Time • Process Steps • Drawings • Samples • APQP File	Evaluate 7 Alternatives • • • Complete Best Processes At A Glance Summary	Evaluate ↓ Kaizen ↓ Simulate	Presentation
P M	3-P Training	Creative Phase Alternatives	Full Scale Mock Up of Cell	Redefine Phase • Operator Cycle Time • Machine Cycle Time • Takt Time/Cycle Time • Process Capacity • STD Work Combination • STD Work Layout • Video • Model Cell Audit	

A 3P kaizen event at Freudenberg NOK follows this schedule, with some of the most intense work on developing and evaluating alternatives occurring Tuesday afternoon and Wednesday morning.

VanWambeke notes that at Freudenberg, team members might look for seven different ways to create a hole in a piece of material. But in addition, in a true 3P event, Vatalaro says, "I would ask the question, does the hole have to be there?" Such true 3P events can take time — rarely as little as five days, he adds.

That doesn't mean the events don't produce benefits for Freudenberg NOK. And in fact, VanWambeke notes, their use is increasing — from 7.5 percent of all kaizen events at the plant in 2000 to 17 percent in 2001.

In describing his company's methodology, VanWambeke noted

What's in a Name?

What does 3P stand for? According to James Vatalaro and other consultants with Productivity, Inc., it means "Pre-Production Planning." Freudenberg NOK says the letters stand for "Production Preparation Process." And Vatalaro says he has also heard another version: "Products, People and Process."

Vatalaro comments that, very often, a company launching a 3P effort will "take great liberty to customize exactly what it stands for." That's fine, he says, so long as there is an understanding of the purpose of 3P — which he describes as "stripping the waste out of product design and process design."

during his Shingo conference presentation that Freudenberg deliberately plans 3P kaizen events with a tight focus on time, with a span of no more than a week. He also said the "breakthrough methodology" of the events involves "creativity before capital," an approach that is "quick and crude vs. slow and elegant," and "lightning fast process planning."

Know What You Are Doing

On one point, the two men agree: 3P is an advanced lean manufacturing process, best attempted by a company that already has lean experience.

In Freudenberg's case, the company began its lean transformation in 1989, but did not become involved in 3P until 1998.

"Beginning the 3P process requires gathering a lot of information that you would already have, but also the use of lean tools such as takt time and process steps," VanWambeke notes.

Vatalaro suggests that 3P is best attempted by a company "that has been on a lean journey for a while, more than three or four years, and has probably demonstrated the ability to implement and maintain 5S very well. Continuous flow and takt time are not new to them, and are something they've been able to implement and sustain." The organization also should have top management commitment and some kind of lean infrastructure, he adds.

Once a company has gotten involved in 3P, he says, "you should use it somewhat frequently to keep it part of the culture."

And that's something businesses should be doing, he states, because "3P is the next productivity leap past one-piece flow."

TAKEAWAYS

- 3P can help build quality and error-proofing into processes, and design products for ease of manufacturing.
- A 3P redesign may involve full-scale mockups and simulations.
- Redesign of both product and process can occur simultaneously in 3P.

6

Equipment Designed through 3P Makes a Small Startup Viable

March 2004

How do you finance a new manufacturing company when your budget is limited, and you don't want to give up ownership to venture capitalists or investors?

First, you plan a small company with appropriate targets for revenues, operating costs and capital spending. Next, you develop specifications for your equipment so it will provide the capacity you need. Finally, and perhaps most importantly, you use the lean technique of 3P to design from scratch equipment that has that capacity and can be built within your budget.

That was the process followed in the creation of Apollo Hardwoods in Kane, Pa., which began production in February of 2004 of cherry wood veneers.

Apollo is different from most companies in the veneer business. It is smaller, and its equipment, designed from scratch, is also smaller. It is vertically integrated. It produces panels that are cut to size for customers, rather than just the industry standard of four feet by eight feet.

There is also one other difference: Apollo was created with a total investment of less than \$2 million — and its owners expect to break even before the end of 2004.

Mockups (top) were used to help design equipment at Apollo Hardwoods. Bottom: A bath tub is brought in to test a method of soaking bark off logs.

"What I have seen a lot of other people do is they think about starting something really large, then figure out how they can accumulate a big pile of money," says Ed Constantine, the founder of Apollo Hardwoods. "They spend for a really long time, and eventually they're breaking even. They spend a lot of time and energy on securing the next round of financing. What we tried to do differently was start small enough so we could fund the business without using external investors. We used our money and some bank money. Then we can concentrate in the startup phase on actually starting the business rather than raising money."

Constantine is also the founder and head of Simpler, a consulting firm that works with businesses to implement lean production. Separate from Simpler, he created a company called Base Point whose purpose is to start new businesses and invest in startups created by other people. Apollo Hardwoods is the first Base Point business.

Keeping It Small

Every new business is based on what its founders believe is a market opportunity. Apollo is based on what Constantine and his partner Brent Lillesand believe is an opportunity in the cherry wood veneer market (see sidebar, page 47).

Having identified the opportunity, they also identified the location for their facility. Kane is "smack in the middle of the world's best cherry logs," Constantine declares. And they decided on the size of the facility: 7,500 square feet. Ground was broken for the building in May 2002. At that time, the partners had a rough idea of how large their equipment might be, but the decision on the building's size was "pretty arbitrary," Constantine notes, adding, "by keeping the footprint that small, we constrained the total assets of the business." However, the property where the facility is located is large enough to accommodate four additional buildings, each the same size as the first, if the company expands.

The cut-to-order nature of Apollo means the company can use a wider range of logs than most veneer makers, including some odd-size or lower quality logs that typically are used for lumber but not veneer. These logs cost less, but also yield less than larger logs.

The loading area of the facility is an opening in the building not much larger than one log. "The nice thing about where we're located, right near the trees, is that it's possible to imagine much more frequent deliveries, or we just go out and get it," says Constantine.

Initially, panels are being made to stock, but plans are to rapidly acquire customers and make panels to order. "If we ever let (make-to-stock panels) creep up to more than 20 percent of the business, we've missed our strategy," he adds.

Setting Specifications

However, what most distinguishes Apollo from its competitors is its unique, built-from-scratch equipment. This was developed through the lean process of 3P, which some experts say stands for pre-production planning, while others say it means production preparation process.

While people differ on the words used, they all agree that 3P is an advanced lean manufacturing method for reviewing product and process design from scratch. It may be conducted within a limited time period, like a kaizen event. It typically involves a review of several different ways of achieving the same result to determine which is best for the operation. It often involves construction of mock-ups and simulations. It may lead to a complete change of the way products are designed or manufactured, which processes are used or how manufacturing cells are set up. In the case of Apollo, it led to veneer-producing equipment that had never existed before.

A lot of planning preceded the 3P events during which equipment was designed. "When we started a 3P event, we starting knowing what the machine needed to produce in terms of volume and quality, and knowing what the machine needed to cost to build, roughly what labor we had to put in, and the footprint. We had a five-day process where we invented machines, and we did it with financial and quality and output targets already defined," Constantine explains.

It also helped that both Constantine and Lillesand are mechanical engineers, although "we had to dust off some books,"

Aviation Landmarks and Expensive Logs

Ed Constantine's inspiration for Apollo Hardwoods came partly from his father, Fred, who spent his career in the hardwood veneer industry.

Before starting Simpler, Ed worked first for Jake Brake and then for The HON Company, where he ran one of HON's plants and then ran its wood furniture division. During his time at HON — where he focused on lean principles and the importance of reducing inventory — he was in the process of obtaining a pilot's license. He studied aviation maps, and would joke with his father that the lumber industry "was the only one where the inventory piles were so big that they were aviation landmarks."

In recent years, he also noted that the price of a cherry log has been increasing while the quality of the logs has been deteriorating — more logs have defects and are not perfectly straight. If the yield of the logs could be increased through more efficient processes, Ed reasoned, that would produce a material cost advantage.

Through discussions with his father over the years, including after his father retired, Ed became convinced that a new, more efficient business could be started in the veneer industry.

Through study of the industry, including the work of a market research firm that his company Base Point hired in 2001, Ed saw practices that he believed could be changed for the better. First, most producers of veneer sell it to someone else who laminates it on to plywood. Constantine believed a more vertically integrated company, which produced not only the veneer but the plywood sheets as well, would be more efficient.

Second, one reason quality logs are scarce is that the industry only produces four-foot-by-eight-foot panels and needs logs capable of producing quality veneer in that size. The market research revealed that customers would be receptive to panels that have already been cut to size — to become a desktop or desk panel, for example.

"The challenge is better flow from the tree all the way to the customer, and better yield," Constantine says. "I tapped Dad's four decades of experience. He understood the veneer side, and I understood wood furniture."

Constantine admits. And when it came to actual construction of the equipment, the company hired an independent equipment maker who Constantine says "was good at converting mock-up ideas into a machine." However, the equipment maker was not intimately involved in the 3P design process. "Sometimes if there are too many people who end up working the details, maybe they will tell you a little too early that certain things can't be done," Constantine notes.

Mike Chamberlain of Simpler described the Apollo efforts at the 2004 AME Annual Conference. He noted how the first step in working with a log is to remove all the bark. A first issue, he said, was to decide what to call that process — debarking, removing, cutting or something else — because terminology can lock people into certain ways of thinking. One way of accomplishing the bark removal was to soak it off. Those involved actually brought a bath-tub into the facility to simulate that process.

Constantine stresses that "you need to be very, very disciplined about the specifications for each piece of machinery — what it needs to do from a capacity point of view, quality and capital costs. In a couple of machines, we overlooked some specifications, which probably added a month or two of debugging (once the machines were built). When we do this again, we'll probably take an extra week of five-day activity."

For example, "in our plywood press, we specified its cycle time, we specified the temperature and the pressure that it needed, but we didn't specify the temperature variation that was accept-able, and we did not specify how fast it had to cycle. We found that if you don't close it fast enough, the glue gets hot before it's squeezed. We had to modify the hydraulic system to speed up the closing time, after the fact.

"On the temperature variation within the platen, we set it at 225 degrees, and we said plus or minus 10 degrees. But we didn't say every point on the plate had to be that temperature. So when we did the grid of thermocouples, we found we had some unusually hot spots. We had to change the way we delivered heat to the plate."

Constantine admits that not every target has been achieved. "The capacity of the plant is limited by one of its machines. It's probably about 20 percent under what the financial targets were," he notes. That's not an issue until the plant achieves a certain level of sales, but "that's a high-priority improvement for this summer," he adds. "We need to crack that with a bolt-on rapid improvement or 3P event to achieve its financial capacity. I have such faith in the process that I know we'll get it."

"Most startups buy equipment off the shelf," he observes. "When they do that, they're spending a lot of money. What we were trying to do is figure out how not to spend as much. If we had bought off the shelf, we probably would have required five times the floor space, and we would have spent five times the money. We would have had more capacity, but more business risk. And we would have needed a lot more financing."

His advice: "Believe in the potential of a small footprint and establish a financial model for revenue level, what profitability you are aiming for and how many dollars you are going to spend on assets. We were targeting a return on key assets. Aim for that target; if you can achieve it, you can finance your own growth."

TAKEAWAYS

- Lean methodologies can reduce the cost and risk of starting a small business.
- Designing new equipment using the 3P method can cost less than buying off the shelf.
- Design specifications must be precise, comprehensive and detailed.

Part II

Improving Flow

OVERVIEW

Achieving the continuous flow that is at the heart of lean manufacturing requires a delicate balance of work processes and staffing. Careful planning and constant adjustment of your processes are all part of achieving that balance.

Takt time – the time available to produce a product based on demand – is the basis for continuous flow. Chapter 7, originally published as a Lean Advisor Q&A column, explains how cell balancing can adjust your processes so that each process step matches your takt time.

Chapter 8, also a Lean Advisor Q&A column, addresses a related problem: What do you when one of your products simply cannot be made within takt time? The answer provided in this chapter is that you may need two takt times, with your schedule adjusted accordingly.

One strategy for improving flow lies not in changing your processes, but in addressing quality issues to reduce or eliminate scrap. Chapter 9 tells the story of ATK Ammunition Group, which adopted this strategy and dramatically boosted capacity.

Chapter 10, a third Q&A column, notes the importance of scheduling work in the proper sequence. This chapter explains that the costs of building out of sequence are often underestimated and provides a way to calculate a sequence performance percentage.

Ford is a company that understands flow can only be optimized when processes are standardized. Chapter 11 describes the automaker's production system, and how standardization of processes actually creates flexibility.

Flow is not just for manufacturing. Chapter 12 tells the story of DCR Systems, an automotive body shop that is gaining an advantage over competitors by applying the concepts of flow to collision repair.

7

Takt Time Can Configure a Cell

May 2004
James Vatalaro

How can we determine the best configuration for a manufacturing cell?

Takt time is a good starting point. When we calculate the takt time of a product, we do more than determine the frequency with which each product will exit the cell to meet demand. We also determine, to a great degree, the configuration of the cell in which the product will be produced.

For example, assume that we are a job shop making a product that requires seven different manual assembly processes. Further assume that we have orders for 10,000 units, and we have 600,000 seconds of production time available to do so. The formula for takt time is available production time divided by demand. In this case, that gives us a takt time for the product of 60 seconds (600,000 seconds divided by 10,000 units), meaning we must produce one product every 60 seconds to satisfy demand.

The cycle times of the seven assembly processes are as follows:

Process a: 50 seconds

Process b: 25 seconds

Process c: 30 seconds

Process d: 110 seconds

Process e: 35 seconds

Process f: 55 seconds

Process g: 25 seconds

The current state process load chart based on the above information would look like this:

A quick analysis of the current state process load chart shows the

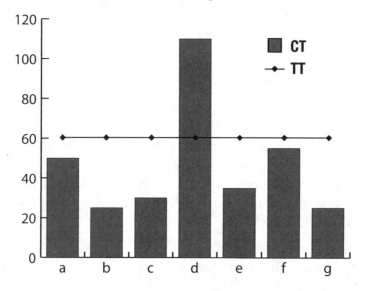

process is not capable of producing to takt time (meaning we may be late on our shipments to the customer) and is filled with significant "takt gaps."

By applying the principles of cell balancing, the work could theoretically be redistributed as shown below in the future state process load chart. This assumes that some operators are willing to be cross-trained and run more than one process. Please note that six operators are required, as opposed to seven for a productivity increase of about 14%.

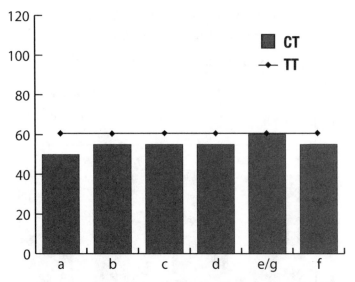

The question is: How does the above future state process load chart, which is designed to accommodate our takt time determination, influence our options regarding cell layout alternatives?

By applying the principles of cell design and one-piece flow, we create a layout for this cell shown in the illustration below.

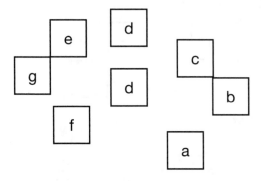

Next, let's assume that we "manage" our takt time. Because we are a job shop, we have a great degree of flexibility in manipulating the numerator of the takt time calculation, available time. Lets assume that we increase our allocation of production time to 900,000 seconds due to a customer delivery date change. Takt time now becomes 90 seconds. What is the impact on the process load chart, and what is the impact on the layout of the cell?

The process load chart could look like this:

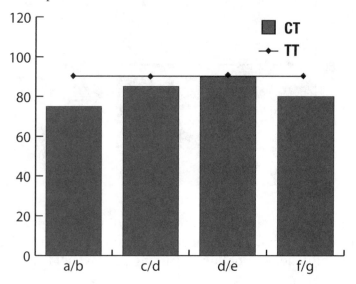

With the processes structured this way, the cell can be redesigned to look like this:

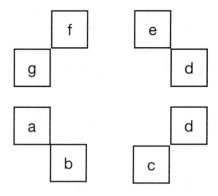

The change is possible because the new configuration of the processes means we only need four operators for production instead of six. In other words, the cell design and the number of operators changed dramatically because we changed takt time.

TAKEAWAYS

- Ideally, each process step within a cell should be producing to takt time.
- Cell balancing can help eliminate "takt gaps" and may also change the number of operators is required.
- Cross-training is often necessary.

8

You May Need Two Takt Times

February 2003
Richard Niedermeier

A product in one of our product families cannot be manufactured within the family's takt time. What do we do?

The metric/baseline of takt time is one of the clearest ones in lean. You take the working seconds in each production day and divide it by the number of units in the product family to be made each day. The resulting number defines the time (in seconds) in which each unit must be produced to meet customer demand. Sounds simple, doesn't it? Yet some of the product families we have put together make the use of the number difficult. Why? It all has to do with the homogeneity of the product family.

Performing a Product-Quantity Analysis for volume and a Routing Analysis for resource/equipment allocation generates the product family membership. This is done to be sure that we have parts similar in their routing pattern and enough volume of them to dedicate the space, the people, and the equipment to the customers' demands. If the product family is highly homogeneous, then the concept's application is clear and simple. A problem can arise if the family of products is not "homogeneous enough."

If the amount of time spent by any work center on one of the family members is drastically different from the majority of the rest of the family members, then a separate takt time for that product needs to be generated.

Here is an example:

A production line requires that 1,000 units be made each day during the 7.2 hours of the working shift. This would generate a takt time of 26 seconds. [7.2 hours equals 432 minutes or 25,920 seconds. Divide by 1,000 units to get takt time.] This will work fine if all of the 1,000 units to be produced have similar production time requirements. [Wooden lead pencils can come in a variety of colors, but the time to paint them is the same regardless of the color used.]

But in this group, there is a product that requires twice as much resource time on the line than any of the other products in the family. In fact, the cycle time of this product exceeds the average takt time by 100%. We need to make 100 of them across the same set of resources. In this case we will need to calculate a separate takt time for this product and rebalance the line load for it.

The way to do this is to take a portion of the working day and allocate it to the production of just this product and to compute the takt time based on the allocated hours. The outcome then is a takt time for the majority of the day at an average of 23 seconds, and a takt time for the 100 units of at least 52 seconds during its allocated production time. [Allocate 5200 seconds for the non-homogenous product (100 units times a takt time of 52 seconds). That leaves 20,720 seconds for the remaining 900 products, or a takt time of 23 seconds.]

After time in the shift is allocated to this product, the accuracy of the allocation needs to be validated. If the original allocation was based on the standards provided from production engineering rather than from observation, this is an essential step. This is more of a scheduling technique than pure takt time application, but it is a real world occurrence.

With the original takt time for the unique part set at 52 seconds, the first scheduling effort would look like the table below:

PARTS/ TIME	Hour 1	Hour 2	Hour 3	Hour 4	Hour 5	Hour 6	Hour 7
Family Group	1	1	1	1	1	.6	
Unique Part						.4	1

After some real world experience, the time allowed for the unique part has been cut to 50 seconds per piece. The new schedule would be:

PARTS/ TIME	Hour 1	Hour 2	Hour 3	Hour 4	Hour 5	Hour 6	Hour 7
Family Group	1	1	1	1	1	.75	
Unique Part						.25	1

The extra time created by reallocating the unique parts would be used to smooth out the average for the other members of the family. This would make the schedule easier to execute. Although the tendency here would be to tighten down to the exact time needed, this would make the execution of it too difficult.

TAKEAWAYS

- If the time required to make one item is drastically different from others in a product family, that product may need a separate takt time.
- Products with different takt times will be made at separate times, not simultaneously.
- The time allocated for each product must be verified.

9

Reducing Scrap Paves the Way for a Big Boost in Capacity

February 2005

When you are seeking ways to increase capacity, you may think about eliminating or shortening the steps in your process. But sometimes, the biggest increase in capacity can be achieved simply through scrap reduction.

That has proven to be true for ATK Ammunition Group, a company that makes small-arms ammunition used by U.S. military forces and has had to quadruple production for the military since 2000. In trying to keep up with those increases in demand, ATK — which is pursuing six sigma strategies and will soon be adding lean approaches as well — has focused initially on scrap reduction.

In 1999, the company won a competitively bid contract to operate the Lake City Army Ammunition Plant, just outside Independence, Mo. The facility, some 400 buildings on about 4,000 acres, is the source of 90 percent of all U.S. military small-caliber ammunition. It is overseen by the U.S. Army Joint Munitions Command, which channels the ammunition produced to all branches of the military.

ATK actually began operating Lake City in April of 2000. (The ammunition group is a subsidiary of Alliant Techsystems, a company created when Honeywell spun off its defense businesses in 1990.) At the time, the complex had about 650 employees and produced 300 million rounds of ammunition per year.

But since then, what ATK spokesman Bryce Hallowell calls a "perfect storm" of three changes in the world have come together to increase demand.

First are the wars in Afghanistan and Iraq. Second, the Army has adopted procedures requiring more extensive training for all soldiers in the use of small arms — meaning more ammunition is needed for training. (Hallowell refers to this as the "Jessica Lynch effect," a reference to the soldier captured and then rescued in Iraq, and the belief by some officials that the capture may have resulted, in part, from U.S. soldiers not being proficient enough in small arms to engage the enemy in more of a firefight.)

Third, the military maintains reserves of ammunition that have been depleted over the last decade — and are now being replenished.

As a result of these factors, the workforce at Lake City — which has grown to 2,000 employees — is now producing 1.2 billion rounds per year, with ATK expecting demand to grow to between 1.5 billion and 1.8 billion by 2006.

And to make the situation even more challenging, ATK was given a fixed-price contract to operate Lake City, in contrast to the cost-plus contracts given past operators. Therefore, containing and lowering costs is essential.

Frequent Rejects

When a six sigma approach was first launched in 2004, the initial focus was on reducing scrap, for the simple reason that "we had thrown away millions of dollars," comments Erich Jahnke, one of two employees at the facility who have become six sigma black belts.

And one of the more interesting results of that focus came during a study of scrap generated on a line producing .50-caliber ammu-

Employees at ATK produce 1.2 billion rounds per year.

nition. Scrap from the line was ultimately reduced by about 50 percent, and one of two major changes leading to that reduction was the addition of a process step.

A significant amount of completed ammunition was being rejected by a machine gauge used at the end of the line. However, team members determined that the machine "was not as effective as we thought," notes Sheryl Parker, the other black belt. "A lot of good work was considered scrap by the machine."

So a more precise hand gauge was added at the very end of the line, to check the ammunition that had been rejected. Many of those rounds were then found to be acceptable, reducing the amount rejected.

But Parker also notes that team members knew up front the addition of the hand gauge would not be the ultimate solution. They hope at a later time to eliminate that gauge, she says, perhaps by improving the machine gauge or improving the inspection process in some other way.

The other major factor reducing scrap on the .50-caliber line was a recognition that a lot of material was being lost because the paperwork authenticating its quality was being lost. And that was happening because ammunition traveled all over the shop floor while being produced — a classic lean spaghetti diagram, according to Parker — creating many opportunities for the paperwork traveling with it to be put down in the wrong place. What Parker calls "a rather significant layout change" addressed that problem.

The layout change actually occurred before the addition of the hand gauge, and made that addition possible by improving production flow.

Another improvement example occurred in a section of the facility making ammunition cases. The scrap rate of the five lines in this section was high, Jahnke says, but a failure mode and effects analysis (FMEA) made clear that most of the scrap was generated by only one line. (FMEA is a format for analyzing failures and generating improvement ideas.) With some small efforts to rebuild machines, improved training of operators and improvements in the way gauges were used to measure parts, variation on the line was cut by about 80 percent, he notes.

Back to Basics

So far, ATK has trained Parker and Jahnke as black belts, plus 30 other people as green belts. In the near future, the company is launching what it calls a "yellow belt" program to train a much larger number of employees in a basic level of six sigma. In addition, the ammunition group has just started to develop plans for implementing the parent company's lean approach, which has the name PES, or production enterprise system.

In 2005, the focus of improvement efforts at Lake City will be shifting from reducing scrap to increasing capacity through other means, such as changes in steps of the manufacturing process.

Director of engineering Debbie Lux says one approach that helps sustain the effort is to have regular reviews of six sigma projects before a group consisting of herself, the quality director, the operations director, the plant manager and other executives so that any "hiccups" can be spotted early. "I think that visibility is absolutely essential," she comments.

"For the most part, people have been very excited about adopting this new technique. They recognize there is a need for a scientific discipline," Lux observes. "I'm a little bit surprised as to how well it's been embraced. People actually ask me, 'When are we going to have the next training session?' There is so much excitement here at the plant."

Parker, who has been at Lake City since before ATK took over, comments, "My personal feeling is we need change. What this has done for me as an engineer is we've gone back to the basics of what we were trained to do. We apply these tools, and I am assured in my own work that I am making the right decisions, and I can go to management with the right information."

TAKEAWAYS

- Good products may be rejected due to poor measurement of quality.
- Products can also be rejected due to missing paperwork.
- Sometimes a process is improved by adding a step.

Building out of Sequence Is Expensive

June 2003
Richard Niedermeier

We plan to build products in a particular sequence, but often find we have to change that sequence. Does this matter?

Yes, it does. Out-of-sequence work — work that was planned and procured for in one order but was actually performed in a different order — is costly in several ways.

This can be seen through "Build to Schedule," one metric that can be applied in a lean environment. This particular metric has three components: volume, mix, and sequence.

Like some other metrics, Build to Schedule or BTS has more than one benefit. Each of its three components can be used to drive continuous improvement in that particular area. In addition, putting the components together in a formula where they can have equal impact on the outcome of the metric's direction turns them into a measurement of a general trend.

In this case the general trend suffers when work is performed out of sequence. As can be seen in the accompanying example, a low percentage of sequence performance drives down the overall BTS performance.

A low sequence performance percentage should also be recognized as an opportunity for improvement, but this opportunity is

Calculating Build to Schedule

The following units were scheduled for Typical Plant yesterday:

Model A	500 units
Model B	300
Model C	200
TOTAL	**1,000 units**

The following units were actually built by Typical Plant yesterday:

Model A	300 units
Model C	100
Model B	650
TOTAL	**1,050 units**

Volume Performance: Volume Performance is 100% (maximum level): 1,050 units were built while 1,000 units were scheduled to be built.

Mix Performance

The Actual Number of Units Built to Mix is:

Model A	300 units	
Model B	300	(overbuild)
Model C	100	
TOTAL	**700 units**	

Mix Performance is 700 ÷ 1,000 = 70%

Sequence Performance

often ignored. The cost to the business in general for out-of-sequence work is usually underestimated. Although the direct costs associated with out-of-sequence work are accounted for, those of an indirect nature are usually ignored or underestimated.

Work is typically performed out of sequence when customer demand changes, materials arrive late or machines break down, for example. The direct costs of out-of-sequence work might include overtime hours required, expedited services, increases in scrap or rework, and expedited transportation. Most computer-based standard cost systems have categories where these can be collected and calculated at a later date.

The indirect costs are rarely considered, but they can be significant. These indirect costs would include clerical time required to update the system regarding delays, orders missed or expedited. In addition, peripheral departments must now be notified of the cascading change through reprinting of production schedules, expediting lists, stock room activity demands, and Kanban system buffers. (Be sure to allow for overhead allocation when collecting these costs.)

You should periodically update the values that you use for the indirect costs — for example, the hourly cost of time spent expediting or rescheduling — throughout the calendar year if for no other reason than to understand the true costs of missing the scheduled due date, or for expediting an order through the system.

TAKEAWAYS

- The cost for out-of-sequence work is usually underestimated.
- Indirect costs are rarely considered, but can be significant.
- The numbers of products built to mix and build to sequence can be used to calculate performance.

11

Ford Sees Its Future in Flexibility

October 2004

The key to making your manufacturing system flexible — meaning able to produce a wide range of products — is to standardize everything within that system.

The parts of a car body, for example, should always be welded together in essentially the same way, no matter what type of car is being made. The tools and equipment used to perform the welding should always be the same.

This type of standardization is at the heart of Ford's new production system. Developed over the last two years and now in use at a handful of Ford plants, the system involves a well-defined global manufacturing process, about 60 process templates for building cars, and a mere 16 standard cells that are used to create all of those templates. The cells themselves are created from only about 300 standard components (see sidebar page 75).

"It was really brought about in response to what we foresaw as the continuing fragmentation of the market," explains William Russo, Ford's director of advanced manufacturing and engineering, adding that "the days of filling even a single plant with 250,000 to 300,000-plus units of common volume of a single model" are essentially gone or disappearing.

"Rather than each body shop being a newly created masterpiece, it

The Ford Five Hundred, Ford Freestyle and Mercury Montego are all built off the same platform and roll off a single line at Ford's Chicago Assembly Plant, which utilizes the company's flexible manufacturing system.

makes it very standard. We are able to shrink the time in engineering, we are able to shrink the fabrication time, we are able to shrink the time it takes to fixture and build up to creating volume," he adds. "We are able to shrink the total amount of time it takes to engineer, fabricate and launch vehicles."

The few Ford plants now using the new system do not, in fact, produce more than two or three different vehicles each. However, the system gives those plants the capability to handle a much greater variety of vehicles, positioning Ford for the future.

Until recently, "quite frankly, Ford didn't have a need to do that. We have a number of plants that are full with one or two models," Russo states. "But we see that changing."

In addition, a standard manufacturing system enables Ford to make cars more rapidly and introduce new models more quickly while simultaneously improving quality.

Templates, Subassemblies and Cells

Ford's global manufacturing system began with the concept that a great deal could be done to standardize the way Ford builds vehicles.

"We sat down with all of the Ford trust brands and agreed on a global manufacturing process," explains Russo. "We really addressed how we wanted to address the various main subassemblies in the body shop. It allowed us to make the sharing of platforms in the future easier. It wouldn't be exact — everybody has his own regional ideas — but it does allow for platforms to be shared more easily, because of the way they go together."

At the highest level, the system consists of about 60 process templates, each of which defines the process for a particular part of a vehicle. "A body side main subassembly would be one process template. A framing system is a process template," Russo explains.

Each process template consists of that subassembly or system going through a series of cells.

There are only 16 cells, and a particular template will use anywhere from 3 to 12 of them, depending on the process.

Each cell is created from components, of which there are about 300.

For example, one cell is what Ford refers to as Cell 12 — a welding cell. It is made up of components that include welding robots, a standard transfer pallet, and so on.

The welding cell might be used in several different process templates. For example, it is used extensively in what is known as a re-spot lane, when the components of a vehicle are held in place while the robots weld them together. It is also used near the end of the main assembly line, to perform final welding.

Another cell performs what is known as dimensional certification. Here the robots use cameras rather than welding devices to verify that all components are present and in the right place.

A key point is that the sequence of the cells will vary from template to template, depending on the process. Creating the right sequence involves what Ford refers to as "shingling." Just as the shingles on a roof must be installed in just the right order, each one on top of the one before it, a vehicle subassembly going through a particular process must pass through the cells of that process in exactly the right order.

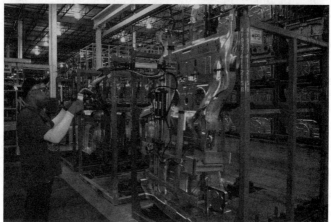

Employees of Plastech Engineered Products assemble a second-row console on the Ford Freestyle (top), while an employee of Tower Automotive loads a rear floor pan onto a delivery rack using a lift assist robot (bottom). Plastech, Tower and 10 other suppliers have employees working at Ford's Chicago Manufacturing Campus, supporting the automaker's nearby Chicago Assembly Plant. (see sidebar, page 77).

"The systems are more robust, from the standpoint of being able to forecast and consistently produce the volume," he explains. "We're seeing far less downtime in our systems. The systems have a higher mean time before repair and a much smaller mean time to repair. We have simplified so much from a maintenance standpoint that they are easier to operate and maintain."

Suppliers Help Support Flexible System

In August of 2004, Ford announced that its flexible manufacturing system had officially gone into operation at its Chicago Assembly Plant. Utilizing the system, the plant is now building three distinct models off one vehicle platform, and it has the capability to build up to eight models off two platforms.

The plant ceased production of the Ford Taurus and Mercury Sable in early 2004. After the conversion and restart, the plant now produces the Ford Five Hundred, the Ford Freestyle and the Mercury Montego.

In addition to implementing the flexible system, Ford also installed extensive new technology in the Chicago Assembly Plant, including laser welding in place of spot welding, in-line machines that inspect and record quality data on all critical body dimensions at a rate of one per hour (versus three per day previously), and a Center of Excellence for checking all components and optimizing part-to-part coordination of the entire vehicle (versus coordination of sheet metal components only in the previous system).

Along with the restart of the plant, Ford also launched its nearby 1.5 million-square-foot Chicago Manufacturing Campus, where 12 suppliers produce parts and logistical support for the assembly plant.

"The flexible manufacturing system installed here means we can respond quickly to changes in customer demand and do so efficiently. And our supplier manufacturing campus supports our flexible manufacturing system with quick customer response time as well as lower inventory and shipping costs," said Greg Smith, executive vice president and president of the Americas for Ford.

Ford spent a total of about $800 million on the plant, the campus and its nearby Chicago Stamping Plant. The three facilities employ a total of 5,600 people. The city of Chicago helped recruit and train 600 new employees for the assembly plant.

In addition, "as we move from model to model, or do a major refreshing, or bring totally new models in, the process is the same, the sequence is the same. Therefore, we build a lot of stability in. While the components they put together may have unique colors or look slightly different, overall they are going to go together in the same sequence and pretty much in the same manner, so we have the opportunity then to continue to improve the quality."

The new system is being rolled out in conjunction with new product launches, meaning the plants that are converted to the system first are those where the new products will be produced. The new Ford F150 was launched recently at the Norfolk plant with the new system, and launches of other new products are set for other plants that have been transformed.

"What you typically see in the industry is that you end up with a quality hit or bump as you introduce new models. What we have proven in the F150 launch and are in the process of, in producing products in Chicago and Flat Rock, is that we are on track to launch these new products at a higher quality level than the previous model," Russo boasts.

Ford intends to convert 80 percent of its plants to the new system by the end of this decade.

TAKEAWAYS

- Enterprise-wide standardization of processes and their components is the key to flexibility.
- The sequence of processes can be varied for different segments of production.
- Flexibility allows for faster introduction of new products and new configurations of old products.

12

Building a Better Body Shop

May 2005

If you launch a new business that implements lean principles more effectively than any competitors, is that a formula for success?

Michael Giarrizzo, Jr. believes it is. His field — auto body repair — is one where lean is largely unknown — something he says gives him an advantage.

His new company DCR Systems, launched at the start of this year, combines utter devotion to lean principles with a business model unusual for his industry. He offers a turnkey operation to auto dealers: A dealer provides him with a location at the dealership. DCR Systems owns and operates the body shop in that location, doing so with what it says is less space, lower cost and higher quality than anyone else. The dealer receives rent payments and a share of profits.

Cleveland-based DCR Systems has one shop in operation so far, another under construction and deals being signed for more.

Giarrizzo, the company's CEO, claims that his type of repair center is better than most other repair shops in several respects. According to Giarrizzo:

- A DCR Systems facility occupies 12,000 square feet (including both production space and offices), while a traditional shop with the same capacity is about two-and-a-half times that size.

- A traditional shop requires about a million dollars worth of

Vehicles being repaired move through a U-shaped cell in half the time of a traditional body shop.

equipment, while his requires less than half that.

- The DCR Systems cycle time to complete a job "keys to keys" is currently 7.2 days, about half the industry average. And "we think we can get it under six," he adds.

On that last point, Giarrizzo also says it should be possible to cut the cycle time in half again since, until now, the repair industry has never been able to operate with multiple shifts. That is because, in traditional collision repair, each vehicle is repaired by one mechanic who works on it from beginning to end — what Giarrizzo calls the "subcontractor mentality." When the mechanic goes home at the end of the day, with the work unfinished, no one else can use his workspace because the vehicle is still sitting there.

In a DCR Systems facility, vehicles being repaired move through a U-shaped cell, and no one worker "owns" a particular vehicle — meaning the work could continue into the next shift.

At a DCR systems facility, a rail line is used to move the vehicle through the repair process.

Long Experience

Giarrizzo formed DCR Systems after literally a lifetime spent in auto service. His grandfather founded a gas station in Ohio in 1946, which his father turned into a repair shop in the 1960s. In 1998, at the height of consolidation in the repair industry, the family agreed to sell the business (which had grown to four shops) to Sterling Auto Body Centers.

The company's COO at the time attempted to apply lean principles to the business, but Giarrizzo says the COO failed to do so effectively. Giarrizzo won backing from the CEO to try his own hand at improving the Ohio locations and ultimately rose to become the new COO — shortly before the business was acquired by Allstate.

But while Giarrizzo continued working after the acquisition to make the company lean, with support from a board member who served as his mentor, "I never felt like we really got the full impact or fundamentally changed the strategic processes," he says.

He left Allstate in late 2003, spent some time consulting and ultimately created his current company.

He believes there is ample opportunity for DCR Systems, stating that 60 percent of the approximately 21,000 auto dealers nationwide do not have body shops, and of the 40 percent who do, "80 percent are not certified."

The Old Way

According to Giarrizzo, the traditional auto body shop is a model of inefficiency. The traditional process begins with a technician writing up an estimate for repair based on the car's appearance. Parts are then ordered, which can take two to three days because some parts may be out of stock.

Once the technician begins work, he may find additional damage not initially visible. When this happens, work stops, the insurance company is contacted, additional parts are ordered and the car is moved out of the repair shop until the additional parts arrive. Once they do, the car is brought back in at the next available time — which may not be right away, because the technician's space may now be occupied with another car. This process is often repeated more than once; Giarrizzo says the industry "has about a 250 percent supplement rate, meaning that for every initial estimate, it takes two-and-a-half more times to get it right."

Once the technician has completed body repairs, the car or its parts may be sent off to a painter. They are returned after the painting is done, and the technician begins re-assembling the vehicle. But his work may be interrupted if he discovers he has a part that is incorrect or broken, which happens because parts are not typically inspected when they first arrive.

Overall, the process takes a "very unpredictable, very unreliable amount of time," Giarrizzo says.

A Better Way

There are numerous differences in the DCR Systems approach. At the outset, workers perform a "strategic disassembly," which means removing any and all parts related to or in conjunction with the damage. This enables workers to see all damage, external and internal, right away, provide a complete estimate and order parts just once.

Part of the strategy involves Giarrizzo getting parts vendors, such as dealers, to guarantee they will ship all parts within 48 hours of receiving the order, thereby making sure the order is 100 percent complete.

That takes some persuasion. "Before they throw you out the door, they tell you you're crazy," he observes.

But Giarrizzo says he convinces dealers by telling them a statistic they may not have heard: The typical repair job involves about six and a half invoices. Thus, if a dealer receives an order for ten parts, only has eight in stock and has to pay overnight shipping charges to obtain and supply the two others, he is still better off because he eliminates the time, cost and aggravation involved in additional invoices.

All parts are removed from boxes and inspected when they first come in. When the workers are ready to begin, the key to making the system work is to remove some of the variability inherent in a business where the amount of repair required can vary tremendously from one job to the next.

This is done by separating out the tasks requiring the most significant work and the most skilled technicians — welding or engine repair, for example. These are taken care of in what is called the "pre-op" area, in a step that is independent of the process flow.

The result is that the vehicle is then ready for what is called "production without interruption." The vehicle then moves along a rail system for work that doesn't require as much skill — e.g., replacement of sheet metal, straightening of sheet metal, preparation for refinishing. Quality verification takes place in between each step of the process.

Giarrizzo stresses that the flow of the vehicle along the rail never reverses, and one vehicle is never leapfrogged ahead of another in the refinishing line, "although in the body line we have flexibility so the faster-moving product can pass the slow-moving product."

With this system, not every worker has to be a skilled mechanic — and skilled mechanics are hard to find. Also, Giarrizzo pays his mechanics a salary, and less skilled workers an hourly wage, in contrast to a traditional shop, which might pay the mechanic a percentage of the rate for each billable hour.

Overall, Giarrizzo says, his system yields "incredible flexibility and a self-directed workforce inside of rigid discipline."

TAKEAWAYS

- Lean can become an advantage in an industry where it is largely unknown.
- Suppliers will do more when they are shown how rework will be eliminated.
- A lean approach can reduce the need for skilled labor.

Part III

Smoothing Production

OVERVIEW

Production inevitably runs into bumps; the never-ending challenge is finding ways to avoid those bumps. Balancing your lines and properly adjusting your production and employee schedules can help achieve that goal.

One important lean tool in this regard is heijunka, or load leveling. Especially with high mix, low volume operations, heijunka can help smooth the day-to-day variations in orders. How Autoliv applies heijunka is described in Chapter 13.

Chapter 14 explains an unusual concept – a self-balancing line. Taking the attitude that traditional line balancing will never achieve optimum performance, managers at an OCLI/JDS Uniphase plant have operators move back and forth among work stations to boost throughput.

Another contrary approach is described in Chapter 15: Managers at Pelican Products abandoned the practice of basing production on the amount of product to be made, and instead use a "train schedule" of when products will be made.

At a Bridgestone/Firestone plant, a more consistent, continuous operation is being achieved through the unusual strategy of scheduling employees to work 12-hour shifts. Read about it in Chapter 16.

13

Heijunka Can Help Eliminate Production Peaks and Valleys

October 2002

At the Autoliv plant in Ogden, Utah, Clay Wilker's goal is to "build a little bit of everything every day."

That can be a challenge for Wilker and other managers at the plant. Autoliv makes inflators for airbags; because there are several types of inflators, and a range of variations for each, the facility produces more than 300 different items.

However, Wilker's goal is important because it represents an important principle of lean manufacturing: Heijunka, also known as load leveling or level scheduling.

Simply put, heijunka is the sequencing of orders in a repetitive pattern of production, aimed at smoothing day-to-day variations in total orders. A term perhaps not as widely known as kanban or kaizen, heijunka is nonetheless equally important because it contributes to inventory reduction and more efficient use of labor.

"Basically, what you achieve is production control," says James Vatalaro, a consultant with Productivity, Inc. "If you are able to produce a product every day, you have true velocity. Your inventory turns are more frequent, you can produce product in lower batch sizes, your cost goes down, your quality goes up."

Heijunka is one of the more advanced concepts of lean production, and not applicable to every situation. "When you have a supplying resource that's responsible for producing multiple products for multiple customers — high mix, low volume — that's where we've seen heijunka work best," Vatalaro says.

He also states, "Don't jump to heijunka right away. A lot of work needs to be done first on the current-state value stream map to get to your future state. Continuous flow production always comes first. When you do a current-state value stream map, the question you should be asking yourself first is not where can we put a kanban system, but where can we put continuous flow. Only after thorough analysis, then we think of the pull system, which is heijunka.

"With that stated, for a company that's been on a lean journey for a while, heijunka might be very appropriate."

A Lot of Fine-Tuning

What made heijunka appropriate for Autoliv (when it was first implemented in the mid 1990s) was that production was being scheduled based on MRP-type forecasts. Variations in forecasts and in customer demand meant that "it seemed like we always didn't have enough of something or too much of another thing," Wilker says. He described their experience with heijunka at 2002's Shingo Prize conference in Kentucky.

To put it another way, he adds, "if we run simply on the orders that come in, because of variation we have a lot of people standing around some days, and other days they have too much to do. We have to staff, and have the amount of equipment, to be able to react to those peaks." The Ogden plant employs about 1,800 people, making about 1.1 million inflators per month.

Applying heijunka involves reviewing many different factors, with a lot of fine-tuning, Wilker notes. At Autoliv, these included looking at finished goods on hand, frequency of shipments (ranging from monthly for European customers to several times a day for some U.S. locations), and the volume and variety of products to be manufactured.

There were also "a lot of small improvements in the way we handle our cards, the way we adjust for how much inventory we have, improvements in the way we transfer information from within our plant to our suppliers," he says.

The effort involved working with customers, where Autoliv had "a little bit of success" getting customers to smooth out their orders. Wilker states: "Our customer reps would talk to our customers and try to get them to understand why their orders were coming in with such variation. They really weren't seeing that kind of variation. The numbers go in the computer, and what ends up coming out with all the different MRP functions kind of messes up the signals sent to us."

One approach that brought a little success, he adds, was in saying "what if we take that average per day and take one part number and just ship that one part number, and not pay attention to the signals." However, when dealing with large automakers, "to get somebody to work with you on a part-by-part basis in our business is very difficult."

Nonetheless, Wilker says heijunka has worked well for Autoliv. An additional benefit has been that "it helps you level out your supply base. They have a more predictable method of how to supply materials to you, so you are not running out of materials and shutting down your production line."

Vatalaro notes that heijunka "is perceived as being difficult." However, he adds, "once you've internalized the basic concepts, by staying true to the principles, then it's not that big of a mystery. The hard part is getting your hand around the principle."

TAKEAWAYS

- Work with other lean principles, including value stream maps, and a focus on continuous flow are necessary before tackling heijunka.
- Heijunka works best in high-mix, low volume operations.
- Goods on hand, frequency of shipments, and volume and variety of goods to be made must all be taken into account.

14

Work Speeds Up As Operators Move

December 2003

How do you balance the work on a production line to achieve a steady, continuous operation?

At the OCLI/JDS Uniphase plant in Santa Rosa, Calif., where they make optical coatings and commercial lasers, the answer is: You don't. Instead, you have the operators move so that there is never an interruption in the flow of production.

At OCLI/JDSU, if the last person on the production line has completed the last operation, that person walks upstream to the next worker and takes over that worker's operation. The displaced worker then bumps the next person up the line, and so on.

This is called a self-balancing line, in which operators follow some unusual practices to ensure that work is continuous (see sidebar, page 92). Gordon Ghirann, continuous improvement facilitator at the plant, is the first to admit that the practice "flies in the face of the Toyota model," which is the foundation for lean manufacturing today. He adds, "It's a totally different paradigm. The Toyota model is based on trying to forever level load and get closer and closer to balanced. Self-balancing is a totally different approach: 'Level loading will never get you balanced.'"

It is also a better approach in some situations, Ghirann maintains, with productivity gains that he says are typically 30 percent or

How Self-Balancing Works

In a self-balancing line, operations are in a progressive sequence, and the number of operators is determined by the desired production rate, limited only by the length of the line. Each operator works in a "position" or general area that encompasses several operations in sequence (see diagram, page 93).

Self-balancing goes on all the time, but each cycle begins when the operator at the very last operation — call him operator X — finishes working on a product and moves it out of his operation. He then moves to the next upstream operation, no matter where it is, and takes over that production process. In doing so, he relieves that operator, who moves upstream and repeats the process with the next upstream operator.

This continues until the last operator upstream (at the beginning of the line) goes to the first operation and begins work on a new product.

Next, when the person who is the furthest downstream — operator X — finishes the work to be done at his operation, he takes the piece and moves to the next operation downstream, continuing the work. (All other operators do the same at their own pace.) This goes on until he finishes at the very last operation. Then the process starts all over again.

more. In one example, he says, OCLI saw a 60 percent gain in productivity (as measured in units per hour per person) with the adoption of self-balancing — and that was in a line where level loading had already been implemented. In one case, a worker was taken off a line to slow it down because self-balancing made it operate too quickly, Ghirann claims.

The increased speed occurs, he explains, because self-balancing eliminates all waiting time and eliminates the problem of the slowest person setting the pace.

Ghirann said his prior company learned the technique from consultants Jack Zimmermann and Ken McGuire. Ghirann described the technique at the 2003 Toronto conference of the Association for Manufacturing Excellence (AME).

Necessary Conditions

Zimmermann — who says he has "retired four times in the last five years" and adds that he is not currently doing consulting work — says self-balancing can be applied to any operation in which parts are assembled or processed progressively. The concept also requires that all operators are walking rather than remaining seated.

Ghirann stresses that self-balancing will work properly only when certain other lean concepts are followed. For example, standardized work is essential. "When you walk upstream to pull from someone, you need to know what's been done and what operation needs to be done next," he explains.

Similarly, handoffs from one operator to another have to be "fairly clean," he adds, taking as little time as possible, especially when takt time is short. And in some cases, there can be a slight wait before a handoff, if the operator who is being bumped is engaged in a process like soldering.

Converting from a sitting line to a walking line is often a challenge due to resistance or physical limitations, Ghirann says, one reason why not all of the lines at OCLI have been converted to self-bal-

Self-Balanced Work Sequence

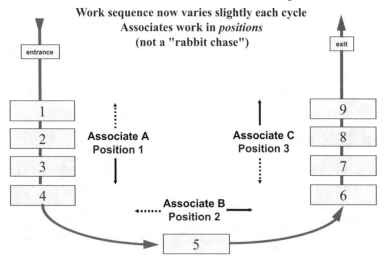

ancing. When the conversion does occur, operators may experience fatigue initially from the constant movement but get used to it in a week or two, according to Ghirann.

And he notes that "it's very important to make the line, and any cell, as compact as possible because the moving is waste, too."

Strong Advocates

Zimmermann claims that he created self-balancing back in the 1980s — by accident. He had helped a client company establish a continuous flow line, but saw the last worker on the line sitting and waiting for the next piece to arrive from upstream. Frustrated by the worker being idle, Zimmerman says he asked the person to go help the person upstream — and self-balancing was born.

Asked why the concept is not more widely known today, Zimmerman replies, "because I didn't write a book. I don't believe in advertising. I was as busy as I wanted to be. There are only a few people who really understand it. It's not always as simple as one would think to adapt to a given environment."

Ghirann suggests that with his presentation at the AME conference, self-balancing "kind of had its coming-out party. There was one member in the audience who knew about it."

Where self-balancing can be implemented, it is superior to level loading, he says, because level loading "kind of hits a wall. You will always have in-process queues, buffers between each operator, because of the fact that you are not truly balanced and never will be balanced. Self-balancing enables you to drain those queues — and they're gone forever. With those barriers removed, teamwork also improves."

TAKEAWAYS

- In a self-balancing line, an operator who completes work moves upstream, bumping the next worker further upstream.
- Self-balancing can produce greater improvement than level loading.
- The length of the line determines the number of operators, each of whom works in an area covering several positions.

Times, Not Products, Set Schedule

December 2004

At Pelican Products, the production schedule doesn't say that X number of products must be made today. It says that a particular machine set up with particular tools to make particular products will run during a certain time period. The number of products to be made is not mentioned.

This "train schedule," as Pelican calls it, is designed to help the company become lean while addressing what executives see as its major constraint: limited capacity caused by lengthy setup times. The schedule stems from use of a constraint-based scheduling system known as every part, every interval.

"My feeling was that the number one gap in implementing pull systems is that we always assume there is infinite capacity," says Steve Hochheiser, IT director at Pelican, which produces high-end plastic cases and other plastic products.

Capacity has been a problem at Pelican. The company's business has been growing rapidly, and, according to Hochheiser, that has created scheduling conflicts and confusion.

"Everybody kept coming back to me, saying 'just reduce the setup and everything will be fine,'" Hochheiser recalls. "We recognized that even if we cut the setup times in half, and in half again later, it would still be a constraint. We had to have an early recognition that setups are going to be a constraint moving forward."

The problem, he explains, is that the injection molding machines at Pelican are set up with extremely heavy, complex tools. Some of the tools are so heavy that they are dropped into the press with a 24-ton crane. (Switching to a different setup system would require a major investment.) Further, only limited numbers of the company's employees are trained to do the setups.

Calculating EPEI

The new scheduling system is based on the scheduling concept of EPEI – every part every interval. EPEI has been described as capacity-based lot sizing.

The formula for calculating intervals per day is

$$\frac{\left(\begin{array}{c}\text{Available}\\\text{production}\\\text{time}\end{array} \times \begin{array}{c}\text{uptime}\\\text{percentage}\end{array}\right) - (\text{daily demand} \times \text{cycle time})}{\text{Changeover time required}}$$

or

$$\frac{\text{Changeover time available}}{\text{Changeover time required}}$$

Specifically, to calculate EPEI, you first determine the total available production time of your resource (a machine or production cell.) For example, if the machine is manned for two eight-hour shifts, or a total of 16 hours, the capacity is:

$$16 \text{ hours/day} \times 60 \text{ minutes/hour} = 960 \text{ minutes/day}$$

Uptime for this machine may only be 90 percent. Therefore, the total capacity available for production and changeovers is:

$$960 \text{ minutes/day} \times 0.90 = 864 \text{ minutes/day}$$

Next calculate the daily demand, meaning the total amount of daily capacity required to cycle parts. Each part's daily requirement is multiplied by its cycle time per piece. The results are totaled for all parts on the machine.

For example, if 12 parts are run on the machine, and the daily demand is 10 each, for a total of 120 parts, and the cycle time is 6 minutes, the total daily cycle time required is:

$$120 \text{ parts/day} \times 6 \text{ minutes/part} = 720 \text{ minutes/day}$$

The top part of the equation then becomes:

$$960 \text{ minutes/day} \times 0.90 - (120 \text{ parts/day} \times 6 \text{ minutes/part}) = 144 \text{ minutes/day}$$

which means there are a total of 144 minutes available for changeovers.

This is followed by determining how much time is actually needed for changeovers. Assume that it takes 10 minutes to change over for each part, or a total of 120 minutes for all 12 parts.

You then divide the available changeover time by the required changeover time, and the equation becomes:

$$\frac{144 \text{ minutes/day}}{120 \text{ minutes/day}} = 1.2$$

This means that each part could be set up and run 1.2 times per day.

The amount of time needed for running each part is the reverse, and is expressed as days per interval. This figure is calculated with the following formula:

$$\frac{\text{Changeover time required}}{(\text{Available production time}) \times \text{uptime percentage} - (\text{daily demand} \times \text{cycle time})}$$

or

$$\frac{120 \text{ minutes/day}}{960 \text{ minutes/day} \times 0.90 - (120 \text{ parts/day} \times 6 \text{ minutes/part})}$$

which yields 0.83 days per interval or the part of the day available for running each part.

Hochheiser refers to an interval calculated from this method as "a batch size expressed as time."

Pelican created an add-on program for its ERP software to translate this method into a daily production schedule. The intent was to integrate EPEI into the ERP application for capacity management and electronically deliver pull signals to the production cell.

As products come off the line, they are scanned and the data is reported back to the ERP application. That information is combined with data about existing stocks and pending orders. A production schedule — the "train schedule" — is created and frozen for 24 hours. The schedule establishes when each machine is operating using particular tools (for a particular part or family of parts made with those tools).

Vendor deliveries, crane availability and personnel schedules are all synchronized with the 24-hour frozen schedule.

Ideally, this system will produce exactly the number of parts required to meet demand. Hochheiser says that if it is time for a production period to end and there are just a few parts left to be made to reach the required number, production will continue until those parts are made.

He also notes that about 60 to 65 percent of Pelican's products are make-to-stock, the other 35 to 40 percent make-to-order. Make-to-order products must be produced in exactly the amounts ordered, while production of make-to-stock items may be more flexible. Therefore, the make-to-order items are typically scheduled in the middle of a shift, Hochheiser says, so that any problems might be pushed to the end of a shift, and "we'll take the hit on the make-to-stock items."

Improvements and Benefits

Pelican is involved in a variety of lean improvement activities, including efforts to reduce setup times, reduce final assembly times, and so on. As operations are improved, the new numbers are entered into the computer scheduling system.

While the new approach is still in its early stages, Hochheiser says it is producing "huge" benefits in the form of higher machine utilization rates, better adherence to schedules, improved on-time delivery, higher inventory turns and increased productivity. Also, Hochheiser says communication has improved and the company's culture is shifting.

"A lot of companies will create a model line, and it's fantastic, and a couple of years later, they still have just the model line," he states. "They haven't been able to extend it. They couldn't quite figure out how to manage capacity. You can't make this work without factoring capacity into the plan."

TAKEAWAYS

- When capacity is a constraint, the principle of every part every interval (EPEI) can help plan production.
- A computer application, ideally tied into an ERP system, is essential for this approach.
- Such an approach should not preclude attempts to increase capacity.

16

12-Hour Shifts Help Tire Plant Achieve Its Lean Objectives

November 2003

Employees at the Bridgestone/Firestone plant in Graniteville, S.C., work rotating 12-hour shifts as part of the plant's overall lean strategy.

Michael Darr, production planning and delivery service leader at the plant, says the schedule reduces the number of shift changeovers and helps achieve a more consistent, continuous operation — the kinds of benefits one expects from a lean initiative.

A lean strategy — including the rotating shifts — has been in place at the plant since it was built in 1996. And it's a strategy that has produced benefits: The facility won the Shingo Prize for Excellence in Manufacturing in 2001 and an *Industry Week* magazine Best Plants Award in 2002, among other honors. The facility also has a track record of improvements in inventory reduction, scrap reduction and other areas.

Days and Nights

The Graniteville plant has been in operation 24 hours a day since it opened, even during the recession of the past few years.

Under the rotating schedule, all employees work both day and night shifts, alternating between three-day and four-day weeks (see diagram). Shifts are actually 12.5 hours long, with an unpaid 30-minute lunch. The extra half-hour means the shifts overlap by 30 minutes, which allows communication between shifts as the changeover occurs.

The company pays overtime for anything more than 40 hours a week. Thus, an employee who works a three-day week of 36 hours gets no overtime, but the four-day week of 48 hours produces a paycheck that includes eight hours of overtime.

The schedule also means that each month, every employee on the schedule gets an entire week off.

Darr notes that the 12-hour shifts were adopted not only to achieve a streamlined operation. The other reason, he says, is "the culture we wanted to create at the plant was one of a lean mindset, but one also of equality or teamwork. We wanted a rotating shift so everyone shared days and nights. There is no difference there."

As a result, there is no pay differential for working a night shift. In fact, Darr says, the plant has only two pay categories: one for operators and one for maintenance workers.

Avoiding Problems

Darr says that fatigue was one of the biggest concerns of managers when the schedule was first adopted. To address that issue, no one works the most repetitive tasks, such as tire inspection, for a full 12

BFSC
Rotation Schedule

	Mon	Tue	Wed	Thu	Fri	Sat	Sun	Mon	Tue	Wed	Thu	Fri	Sat	Sun	Mon	Tue	Wed	Thu	Fri	Sat	Sun	Mon	Tue	Wed	Thu	Fri	Sat	Sun
A Crew	D	D	D	D	-	-	-	-	-	-	-	N	N	N	N	-	-	-	D	D	D	-	N	N	N	-	-	-
B Crew	-	N	N	N	-	-	-	D	D	D	D	-	-	-	-	-	-	-	N	N	N	-	-	-	D	D	D	-
C Crew	N	-	-	-	D	D	D	-	N	N	N	-	-	-	D	D	D	D	-	-	-	-	-	-	-	N	N	N
D Crew	-	-	-	-	N	N	N	N	-	-	-	D	D	D	-	N	N	N	-	-	-	D	D	D	D	-	-	-

D = Day Shift N = Night Shift - = Off

Work Hours

12 Hours 30 Minutes Shift (with 30 minutes unpaid lunch)
Day   6:45 AM - 7:15 PM
Night 6:45 PM - 7:15 AM

hours. Instead, they will transfer to a different job for part of their shift.

Darr concedes that "the downside, like with any rotating shift, is that you are not consistently going home to your kids every night. You're constantly moving back and forth (between day and night shifts)." However, he adds that the schedule has been generally well-received by employees and "it has not been an exit-interview reason for leaving." But he also admits that the schedule was in place from the day the plant opened; converting to a rotating schedule at an existing plant could be more difficult.

Graniteville is a non-union plant, but Darr notes, "we have some union plants that run the same schedule now."

Bridgestone/Firestone also provides financial planning advice to employees because of "concern that people might take too many vacations. Some people don't know what do with seven days off," Darr says. But he adds that the service was a pro-active move on the part of the company, commenting, "I don't know if it's ever been a problem for anybody."

TAKEAWAYS

- 12-hour shifts can achieve a more consistent, continuous operation.
- Employees work three- or four-day weeks, rotating their schedules.
- To avoid fatigue, no one works the most repetitive tasks for a full 12 hours.

Part IV

Shortening Changeovers

OVERVIEW

Changeovers are one of the biggest production bumps facing any manufacturer, simply because production ceases while machine tools are changed. Reducing changeover time through the lean tool SMED – single minute exchange of die – is thus a valuable approach to improving flow.

One key aspect of SMED is determining which changeover steps can be eliminated or undertaken in advance. How Merck put this and other SMED principles to use is detailed in Chapter 17.

Chapter 18 tells the story of Small Parts, a company that doubled its output through SMED. The techniques used include such simple concepts as having tools more accessible to the operator and establishing reference points on machines.

One often-overlooked aspect of changeovers is how much they cost – and how much can be saved when changeover time is reduced. Chapter 19 provides a framework for calculating changeover costs and explains how that can convince management of the value of SMED.

Different changeovers take different amounts of time; applying that knowledge can determine the order in which products should be made, so that you achieve the optimum sequence of changeovers. Chapter 20 describes the success of Southcorp Wines in embracing that concept.

Finally, Chapter 21 focuses on the importance of mockups and simulations in improving changeovers. Read how Kodak uses these techniques to verify planned improvements, thereby avoiding errors and unnecessary costs when altering equipment.

17

What Is in Your Changeover? Probably More Than You Need

October 2004

Some of the steps in your changeover process may not be necessary, and others may involve actions you can take outside of the actual changeover period. By identifying these types of steps and acting on that information, you can dramatically reduce changeover time.

At the Wilson, N.C. manufacturing division of Merck, the pharmaceutical company applied those principles as part of an effort to reduce changeover time in its packaging process. The project cut typical changeover time from 210 minutes to 75 minutes, a reduction of 65 percent achieved without adding facilities, spending new funds or reducing quality.

With about 100 changeovers performed each year, the savings total about 200 hours per year, or approximately 25 eight-hour shifts. Moreover, those savings occurred on just one of the plant's 16 packaging lines. As Merck works to improve the other lines, even more dramatic savings are possible.

The changeover problem was tackled by a three-person project team from North Carolina State University, and it provided benefits for at least one member of that team. Aditya Shah, a research

Schedule Building — Activity Schedule

OPERATOR 1 — FINISHING POSITION

Task	Time
Backend Status Indicator to RED; Remove Batch Id	00:15
CLEAR INT PRINTER ○ Remove label roll and place in cage ○ Stick last printed label on the Order to Package	5:00 (5:15)
EMPTY BINS & MOVE TO THE SIDE	3:30 (8:45)
BACKEND CLEAN	
1. Visually Inspect ECONOSEAL – Remove Lot and Exp plates	
2. CHECK WEIGHER	
3. OVERHEAD CONVEYORS	14:00 (22:45)
4. CASE PACKER – Blowdown critical areas Remove tablets & blister cards from remaining packages	
5. PALLETIZER – Reset packer counter	
6. COMPONENT STAGING AREA	
SIGN FOR FIRST BACKEND CLEAN	1:00 (23:45)
SWEEP PACKING AREA	4:30 (28:15)
WAIT FOR 1ST FILLROOM BLOWDOWN	

OPERATOR 2 — FILLROOM POSITION

Task	Time
Fillroom Status Indicator to RED; Remove Batch Id	00:15
RECORD GOOD/BAD blisters information	1:00 (1:15)
TAKE PRINT MAT OUT ○ Place base plate in cage	2:00 (3:15)
PULL PUNCH STATION OUT	5:30 (8:45)
REMOVE SLIDE BAR CHAIN COVER ○ Rotate slide bar to remove blisters	3:00 (11:45)
REMOVE BLISTER CARDS ○ From under the PUNCH STATION	1:30 (13:15)
MOVE MATS & BINS TO SIDE	1:00 (14:15)
VACUUM FEEDER	3:00 (17:15)
FIRST FILLROOM BLOWDOWN ○ Blowdown Critical Areas ○ Visually Inspect	10:00 (27:15)
SIGN FOR FIRST FILLROOM CLEAN	1:00 (28:15)

OPERATOR 3 — PACKING POSITION

Task	Time
CLICK ON PARSEC SCREEN-TCU/CO START	00:15
BLOWDOWN ATU ○ Blowdown Critical Areas ○ Add blisters to EH&S/trash ○ Visually Inspect	8:00 (8:15)
BLOWDOWN FLOW WRAPPER ○ Remove Cross Seal Jaw guard ○ Blowdown Critical Areas ○ Remove film from HSM vacuum bag ○ Add blisters to EH&S/trash ○ Visually Inspect	8:00 (16:15)
BLOWDOWN CARTONER ○ Remove Cartoner Lowerator cover ○ Blowdown Critical Areas ○ Add blisters to EH&S/trash ○ Visually Inspect	12:00 (28:15)

assistant pursuing his master's degree was working with Merck as a coop student. After graduating, he was hired by Merck full-time.

Industry Issues

Reducing changeover time was important to Merck because of the way its industry has evolved. New marketing strategies have resulted in more products and more configurations of individual products, each with its own packaging. With more products — and, typically, smaller volumes for each individual product — the number of changeovers is increasing. In addition, increased competition means the payoff from research is diminishing, creating added pressure to reduce costs.

Moreover, the Merck plant did not appear to be very efficient. The project team found that the plant was actually running slightly less than 50 percent of the time. Operations ceased about 21 percent of the time due to unplanned downtime, and about 30 percent of the time due to planned downtime.

At least one source of the problem was immediately apparent, and it had nothing to do with the changeover process. All packaging workers took their breaks and lunches at the same time, which meant planned downtime could be cut significantly simply by staggering the breaks and lunches.

The project team narrowed its focus to reducing planned downtime by reducing changeover time. That involved gaining an understanding of particular features of the industry.

Changeovers in pharmaceutical packaging are different from those of many other types of manufacturing because "the big problem is cleanup, not setup," Shah notes. Before a new product can be packaged, every trace of the previous product must be scrubbed away from the packaging equipment to prevent the wrong drug from getting into the wrong package.

In fact, when the university project team studied the changeover process at Merck, they found that 75 percent of the changeover steps involved cleaning.

That percentage involved a significant number of actions, as the team discovered that a changeover involved 400 separate steps.

Classification and More

The key to getting a handle on such a complex situation was to classify every step into one of three categories: necessary to the process, necessary but capable of being done outside the actual changeover time, and unnecessary.

Classification was achieved through a series of questions aimed at determining why each step was done, who should perform it and when it should be performed.

The result was that 124 of the 400 steps, or 31 percent, were deemed to be unnecessary, and were eliminated. These included redundant component checks, attaching and removing batch identification tags to equipment, and so on.

Another 148 activities, or 37 percent, were rescheduled to take place outside the changeover period. These ranged from ink tray cleanup to material staging to certain paperwork and housekeeping.

Changes were also made in the way some cleanup tasks were approached. For example, in some cases, cleaning involved spraying the whole line to remove traces of previous drugs. This practice was modified so that only critical areas — those where tablets accumulated or got stuck, for instance — were sprayed, saving time.

In another example, the method for removing residual dust from some equipment was changed from blowing to vacuuming, reducing the risk of spraying dust on to some other area of the equipment.

However, these steps were only part of the improvement process. A series of further steps followed, including:

- Development of changeover standards and training of all pro- duction associates to follow those standards.

- Development of activity schedules to reduce changeover time by strategically organizing the internal activities among changeover personnel.

The focus of the effort to design schedules was what those involved called the critical path, meaning those internal tasks that have to be done for the line to be back up and producing. The overall goal was to develop a standardized, achievable process.

And then the new process had to be tested. "Testing is the toughest phase of the process," Shah notes. "The first test is always a mess."

Testing involved measuring the times and the sequence of all activities to make sure the new process was comfortable for the operators. In addition, the line was checked for quality, to make sure quality was not compromised by the new process. Testing also served as an opportunity for all people involved to understand their roles in the new changeover process. Following testing, standard operating procedures were updated.

Another training phase followed, aimed at creating a new routine. Its purpose was to ensure that line teams understood the schedules and external lists, and could perform the changeovers properly. The focus was on quality and safety, not on times, because it was assumed those would improve as people moved up the learning curve.

The project team notes that to successfully achieve these kinds of improvements and to sustain them, several elements are essential, including:

- Having an organizational structure in place to track and correct deviations in the process.
- Regularly conducting further efforts to make the improvement process continuous.
- Strong leadership from senior management, as well as at every other level.

TAKEAWAYS

- Classifying changeover steps can identify opportunities for improvement.
- Standardizing steps and properly organizing activities yields significant gains.
- New processes must be tested to verify improvements.

18

SMED Doubles Parts Output For Metal Stamping Company

October 2003

Brian Hipp, senior lean manufacturing engineer for Small Parts, Inc., recalls how surprised everyone was upon viewing a videotape of the changeover process for one of the company's metal stamping machines.

"The first thing that grabbed everyone's attention was how many times the technician was away from the machine," he remembers. "Where did he go? He went to get a tool. He would walk from one side of the machine to the other. Everybody just had their mouths hanging open."

The process was recorded not to provide entertainment, but to help workers improve the changeover process. That effort was launched because, for a company like Small Parts based in Logansport, Ind., improvements in changeovers can be significant.

Changing over a standard punch press takes an average of three hours. For a more complicated multi-slide machine, the range is 8 to 20 hours. And with 900 active SKUs, about 10 percent of which change each year, Small Parts workers perform a lot of changeovers.

The company's lean efforts revolve around the concept of SMED – single minute exchange of die, meaning techniques aimed at reducing a given machine's changeover time to less than 10 minutes. That goal hasn't been achieved yet at Small Parts, but the results so far have been dramatic nonetheless.

"We've doubled the number of parts we can put on in a given week, and on-time delivery has gone from the mid-80s to the mid-90s in percentage – and it's still climbing," boasts Morris Roeder, director, advance engineering.

One fact that makes the improvements particularly striking is that Small Parts had to find ways to improve some processes without any guidance. While there is plenty of material published about SMED for punch presses, including works by Shigeo Shingo, there is nothing about applying SMED to multi-slide machines, Roeder says — adding that those machines account for about 20 percent of all metal stamping work.

"You could have as many as four, six, or eight pieces of precision-made steel that have to be located in exact positions, so the setup on a multi-slide is infinitely more complicated than on a punch press," he notes. "As a result, nobody has really studied that."

Making It Easy

Improving changeovers involves, at least in part, making sure that the operator has what he needs when and where he needs it.

For example, by locating parts and tools closer to the multi-slide machine, Small Parts managers decreased the number of trips away from the machine from almost 100 down to about 20. The changes included putting the required nuts and bolts in a rack by the machine, rather than storing them in another location, and placing 15 to 20 components required for a setup on a cart next to the machine.

Tools had been stored in a four-foot-high rolling toolbox. However, a review of the process determined that the tools actually needed for the changeover would fit on a two-foot-by-three-foot shadow board – so that's exactly what was created near the machine.

Other changes were designed to make the process easier. By creating reference points on the machine, technicians could more easily put components into place. "It's very crude, very elementary, almost laughable in its simplicity, but it sped up the whole process," says Roeder. "The technician did not have to go into the toolbox and get all these fancy micrometers. [The reference points] got within five percent of the final dimensions. Set-up time improved dramatically."

Since the company makes small parts, its stamping machines are relatively small – about the size of a car engine, for example. Because of that, changeovers were traditionally thought of as a one-person process. However, Hipp changed some parts of the process to two-man operations. By having two people working on opposite sides of the machine, additional hours were shaved off set-up time.

A Continuing Journey

Small Parts was drawn into a lean strategy by its customers. in 2001, Roeder says, a customer invited Small Parts managers to be part of a lean training program they were conducting; Roeder and Hipp attended. Then one of Small Parts' Japanese customers invited the supplier to send people to its lean training programs on an ongoing basis. About 45 Small Parts employees (out of a workforce of 300) have attended so far, many of them supervisors. "It's been an eye-opener for everybody that's gone through it," Roeder says.

He adds that his company's CEO has given strong support to the lean initiatives, making it easier to spread the lean gospel.

A number of pilot initiatives were tried first at a small plant the company has in Monticello, Ind. Their success over an initial nine-month period led to initiatives at the main plant in Logansport. Small Parts also has two manufacturing sites in Mexico.

SMED is not the only lean concept the company is implementing. Another is creating families of parts that can all be made in the same manufacturing cell.

One big project now in its final stages involves applying lean concepts to shipping operations. That's essential, Roeder says, because "in the modern world of automotive, the truck arrives at the dock and will be there for 30 minutes, and if you're not ready, they're gone and you've missed a shipment."

The company owns one of its suppliers, a metal distributor, and is working with that company to implement a pull system.

Hipp is also looking at ways to improve flow on the shop floor, and to eliminate bottlenecks so that queues, or staging areas, don't overflow with inventory. "It's a signal to the rest of the plant that if a queue or staging area is full, that department needs help," he says. "In theory, there should be no need to produce parts any faster than required."

Roeder adds, "Probably a year ago, terms like theory of constraints and bottleneck were unknown terms to us in the stamping industry. Now we are becoming more sophisticated."

Small Parts is also implementing a wireless radio frequency system for data collection, which "keeps people from having to find a computer," Hipp notes.

And the company is trying to improve its process of die maintenance, meaning maintenance performed on a die after it comes off a machine to make sure it will be ready the next time it is needed.

"We are now two years into our lean journey, and we're at that point of investing the lean culture on to the shop floor," says Roeder. "It started with the CEO, then down to the managers and supervisors. We've engaged certain people in lean and kaizen activities. Now we really need to make the lean culture part of what we do every day on the shop floor. That's the focus for us."

Hipp adds, "Having (shop floor workers) involved does not necessarily guarantee they've embraced the culture of lean. I think we'll get there. I couldn't exactly tell you how, but we're going to get there."

TAKEAWAYS

- SMED involves making sure the operator has what he needs when and where he needs it.
- Reference points on machines can make it easier to put parts into place.
- Increasing the number of people performing a changeover may increase efficiency.

19

Calculating Changeover Costs Reveals Potential for Savings

August 2005

Most companies don't calculate what changeovers cost them, and therefore don't realize that reducing changeover time can save huge amounts of money.

That's what John Henry argues, and he is on a campaign to help companies recognize and achieve those savings. It is also his business: Henry is a consultant whose Puerto Rico-based company — Changeover.com — works with businesses to improve changeover time.

Reducing the time it takes for changeovers is a fundamental lean concept. But Henry contends that while most lean companies support that concept, they usually don't give it high priority, partly because they don't calculate changeover cost.

"Very few companies measure it at all," he says, adding that when he speaks at conferences, he'll ask those in the audience to raise their hands if they calculate changeover costs, and "I'm surprised if I get 25 percent of the people there."

But measuring the cost is important, Henry argues, for several reasons. First, he comments, "whether you calculate it or not, the cost exists, and if you don't calculate it, you won't know how important it is."

Further, since reducing changeover time sometimes involves spending money, "you need to know what the cost reductions will be as a result of having expended that money. If I'm going to spend $10,000 on reducing changeovers, what's the benefit?"

(However, Henry adds that most changeover reductions can be achieved with relatively small investments.)

Similarly, the calculation is necessary to persuade top management to fund the reduction effort. For example, if you say that the effort will reduce changeover time by 15 minutes per day, "they have to have a way to evaluate that," he states. "Unless you can convert those minutes to dollars, it's impossible to do an evaluation. If you don't have a good answer (to management questions about benefits), you're not going to get the funding necessary. And you're also not going to get the recognition."

But perhaps the strongest argument in favor of calculating changeover costs is that they tend to be higher than many people realize. Henry says that for companies he has worked with, including a number of large companies making packaged consumer goods, "changeovers fall in the $10,000-to-$20,000-an-hour range."

Therefore, "If the cost is, say, $15,000 an hour, and you can reduce changeover time by 10 or 15 minutes a day, you are talking some big bucks by the end of the year."

Tangible Costs

Henry classifies changeover costs as "tangible" and "intangible."

"Tangible generally means you can express them in dollars with some degree of precision," he explains. "With intangible costs, you realize there is a cost, but it is difficult if not impossible to calculate how many dollars it is."

Incidentally, Henry strongly recommends that the accounting department be involved in calculating changeover costs. "An engineering number isn't an official company number; management is always going to have some doubts (about an engineering number)," he states. "I tell people to get accounting involved."

Lost production is probably the biggest tangible cost, Henry says.

A similar tangible cost is **lost capacity.** He explains, "Sometimes you are running at 100 percent capacity, and marketing says 'we could sell more products if you could make them.' If you reduce changeover time, you gain some additional capacity for free. It's almost the same thing, just a different way of looking at it."

Cost of inventory is another tangible cost. "One of the ways people try to reduce changeover costs is by reducing the number of changeovers with larger production runs," which builds up inventory, Henry comments. Typically, the cost of carrying inventory — the capital that is tied up, warehouse space, labor to maintain and operate the warehouse — is equal to about 30 percent of the value of that inventory, he says, adding, "I tell people it's a 30-percent interest rate."

There are also **direct labor expenses** for changeovers, meaning the hourly cost of the workers conducting the changeover — "not their hourly paycheck, but their hourly cost, which may be double," Henry stresses.

(He notes that during a long changeover, operators may be moved to work elsewhere while mechanics perform the changeover. When changeover time is reduced, the operators may simply stand nearby, idle, while the changeover is conducted, which may seem to increase labor costs. "One of the things I tell people is that they have got to get the operators doing changeovers rather than mechanics, or at least assisting," says. Henry.)

Another tangible cost involves **rejects**. Henry explains, "If you don't do a good changeover, you will have a long startup time before it settles down and runs right. During that time, you usually have a lot of rejects."

Intangible Costs

There are also intangible costs.

"The biggest one is probably going to be **response to your customers**," says Henry. "If Wal-Mart calls up on Monday and says 'those widgets are selling really good. We need another 25 truckloads,' you can't really tell them you can't do it because of changeover problems."

There is also the risk of **reduced market share**. Henry comments, "This sort of goes back to lost production. If you are not producing everything the market wants, you may lose market share. It's really more of a long-term strategic cost."

Stress is another intangible cost, on both people and machines. "With long changeover times, there tends to be more pressure: 'Get the line back up and running!'" he says. "You are pushing your machines harder, and as you push both people and machines harder, they tend to be prone to errors and problems and reduced productivity."

Finally, there may be an intangible cost of **lost innovation**. According to Henry, "If you are running flat out, you don't have any time to stop and think. You are not going to come up with new ideas, or new processes, or ways to improve the product. So innovation suffers."

Henry, who calls himself a "changeover wizard," claims that he likes to promote changeover improvement "because I'm lazy." In presentations he gives about changeover reduction, he says, he has a slide that reads, "Be lazy. Look for easy ways to do things."

TAKEAWAYS

- Changeover cost figures can justify improvement efforts.
- Many tangible costs can be calculated.
- Intangible costs should also be considered.

20

Sequencing Products Leads To Least Changeover Time

August 2003

Minimizing changeover time involves more than just reducing the time it takes to change over a machine. It also involves scheduling changeovers in the right order.

That's the lesson to be learned from the experience of Southcorp Wines, a wine bottler located in the Barossa Valley of South Australia.

The concept is not new, and it's fairly simple: Determine how long each changeover takes. Recognize that some changeovers take longer than others. Then calculate the optimal production sequence; typically, this means that those products that would be followed by the longest changeover times are produced last (see example).

Bernard Zanic, manufacturing systems engineer at Southcorp, says he created the company's "changeover matrix" in 1997 using relatively simple information technology.

That effort has produced a very real benefit. Southcorp's four plants, each employing from 250 to 400 people, typically operate five days a week. Output — before use of the matrix — is about 5,000 cases per day. By optimizing changeover time, Zanic says, Southcorp gets extra uptime that makes it possible to produce an extra 500 cases per day, or 2,500 per week.

Changeovers By the Numbers

On a production line at Southcorp Wines, a particular type of bottle will be filled with a specific wine, topped with a particular cork and then marked with a particular label.

To optimize changeover times, the company first determined the length of each changeover.

In this example, the changeover from Bottle 1 to Bottle 2 takes 30 minutes, Bottle 2 to Bottle 3 takes five minutes, and Bottle 1 to Bottle 3 takes 15 minutes.

Cork 1 to Cork 2 takes 10 minutes. Label 1 to Label 2 takes 45 minutes, and Label 2 to Label 3 takes 10 minutes. From Red to White wine takes three hours, and from White to Red wine takes 30 minutes, etc. Assume that the production schedule calls for three products:
- Product A, which includes Bottle 1, Red Wine, Cork 1 and Label 1.
- Product B, with Bottle 2, White Wine, Cork 2 and Label 2.
- Product C, with Bottle 3, White Wine, Cork 1 and Label 3.

The changeover matrix calculator creates a product-to-product changeover matrix:

	TO		
FROM	A	B	C
A	-	180	180
B	45	-	10
C	30	10	-

The optimal sequence would then be B to C to A, which is equal to (B to C) + (C to A), or 10 minutes plus 30 minutes, or 40 minutes of total changeover time.

The worst scenario would be any sequence where product A is not last.

Southcorp deals with about 400 different items that are made into 1,200 products. To make the matrix work, the company has recorded changeover data on all 1,200 products by starting with all items in the bill of materials.

Currently, the data are stored in Excel files that are used by the matrix calculator software developed in-house. Southcorp uses an

ERP system from SAP. The company has begun a project to standardize all descriptions in bills of materials, which will make it possible to have the SAP system automatically load data into the matrix calculator.

Southcorp is also involved in other lean initiatives, including establishing takt time reporting and efforts to reduce bottling batch size to reduce lead time.

The matrix actually was created after a victory that turned into defeat. A few months after a changeover time reduction initiative in 1997, Southcorp entered a machine changeover competition sponsored by the South Australian Centre for Manufacturing. Workers at Southcorp had taken an old labeling machine, spent about $200 on parts and reduced the changeover time from an hour and 5 minutes to 4 minutes and 27 seconds. They won the competition.

Then, Zanic explains, "high on the win, we attempted a plant-wide initiative. It failed abysmally. Persistent as ever, I tackled the changeover dilemma from the planning end."

TAKEAWAYS

- Scheduling changeovers in the right order can help reduce changeover time.
- Changeover data must be recorded for all products manufactured.
- The product requiring the longest changeover time will often be made last.

21

Success with Cardboard & Duct Tape

June 2004

One of the best ways to attack lengthy setup times for your equipment is to arm yourself with cardboard, duct tape and a pair of scissors.

That's what Tom Warda of Kodak will tell you. A Kodak Operating System manager in the company's color paper and imaging chemicals division, he travels around the world preaching his unique gospel.

Cardboard and duct tape — "my favorite materials. Don't all guys have them?" he asks — are, in fact, an example of his philosophy regarding setup reduction. Warda, who has been involved with setup reduction for since 1990, believes (and says Kodak can demonstrate) that reducing setup times not only increases production time, but also improves quality and reduces scrap. He also believes that simplification is the best route to shorter setup times, and that the best way to test a new design for equipment is to build a model with cheap materials.

At Kodak, "a lot of our equipment, because of the process, is made out of special materials — stainless steel and titanium. We have the stainless and titanium mentality — everything has to be made out of them. They're notoriously hard to work with. Making new equipment costs a lot of money and takes a long time. The beauty of mocking something up is to see if even conceptually it can work. You'd be absolutely amazed at what you can make out of that stuff.

How did Kodak teams find a better atlernative to this cumbersome, 67-pound hopper? See the sidebar on page 124.

You can make some fabulous, fully functional models and try something out for relatively low cost before you go cut the stainless and titanium."

One of Warda's favorite examples involves design of a new hopper to feed chemicals into large reactors (see sidebar, page 124).

Rules of Reduction

However, making cheap mockups is only one part of Kodak's setup philosophy, and not the first part. It follows a series of rules for reducing setup times, which the company says can guide you to greater flexibility.

The first rule originally came from Shigeo Shingo, a key developer of the Toyota Production System: **Shift internal activities to external**. By shifting setup activities so they can be done in advance while a machine is still operating, the actual changeover can occur more quickly.

Second, **eliminate, simplify, automate — only in that order**. Warda stresses that the best form of setup reduction is the total elimination of steps. "If you absolutely have to do something, make it simple," he states. And automation should be used only to gain process control. "We always used to jump right to automate," he recalls. "We've learned that eliminate and simplify is where it's at."

Warda recalls an example of a machine where a lead screw had to be turned with a wrench 26 times to shift from production of one product to another. One solution discussed was use of an air wrench that would make it possible to turn the screw more quickly. However, one of the machine's operators "found a position about 13 turns up that worked for both products, and you never had to turn the crank again," Warda notes. "That's the power of 'don't automate it.'"

The third rule stresses the importance of standard work — not just in actual production, but also in changeovers: **One way, the right way, the same way — every time**. The point, Warda says, is that "if it can be done differently — it will be done differently."

And he recommends that engineers **build the required level of precision into the system — not the setup**.

"It's all about adjustments," he comments. "The goal in any of our setups is one touch." Adjustments mean variability, so unnecessary adjustments should be eliminated, and required adjustments should be converted to settings.

People and Pam

Beyond the setup reduction rules, Warda stresses that with changeovers, as with any lean initiative, having operators involved is crucial.

"If you train your people right and let them come up with a solution, it will not only be better than anything your managers and engineers will come up with, but it will stick because it's theirs.

129

The Heavy Hopper

Kodak has large reactors — about two stories tall — that combine raw materials to produce chemicals. For each new batch, a hatch at the top of the reactor is opened, a hopper (which functions like a large funnel) is attached, the raw materials are poured in, the hopper is removed and the hatch is sealed.

The company was using four different styles of hoppers, each of which weighed up to 67 pounds. They contained numerous parts, were expensive to build, heavy and difficult to move, and difficult to maintain.

A kaizen team tackled the problem with three sub-teams. Their mission was to come up with one style that would fit all reactors and that was simpler to build, easier to maintain, and lighter.

Each team was given a supply of cardboard, duct tape and scissors. Each came back with a model of a new design, and there was "one really good thing" about each design, Warda explains. Those

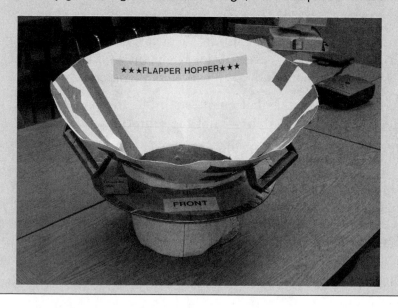

You've got to stand back and get out of the way."

It's also important that the reasons for setup reductions be consistent with overall lean principles. Warda says Kodak used to seek

three qualities were incorporated into a single new design (shown on page 124).

The teams were then asked to go on the shop floor and test each mockup on actual reactors. While they couldn't actually pour raw chemicals through it, they were able to confirm — in the course of three visits to the shop floor — that the new model fit all reactors and could be attached and removed as intended.

The model actually contained more than cardboard and duct tape. One of its features was a flap that closed as material was poured in to prevent leakage. The flap required a counterweight, which on the model consisted of cardboard filled with nuts and bolts.

Following the testing, a functioning hopper prototype was created from stainless steel (below) — weighing only 28 pounds, meaning it was 57 percent lighter, and it cost 70 percent less.
"The really neat thing was that, when they went to make a real prototype, all they did was cut ours up and they had a pattern for it," Warda beams.

reductions in setups for the wrong reason: "In the past we did what a lot of companies did. We worked on reducing setup times, then took that time and used it to make a bigger batch. Now we reduce batch size."

Another key concept is that setups should be practiced. "Even the best pit crews constantly practice their pit stops," Warda notes. He also recommends that a debriefing and critique should take place immediately after each practice, and that a "practice tee" can be built — with cardboard and duct tape. "Spend big bucks as the very last resort," he stresses.

The overriding concept is simplicity. "I have never seen a repeatable, quicker setup that was more complex than the baseline," he declares, though he adds that "sometimes 'simple' takes some thought."

Incidentally, cardboard and duct tape are not the only materials Warda likes. He also recommends using spray paint, magnets, electrical tape, Magic Markers, aluminum, spray foam insulation, Saran Wrap and Pam cooking spray.

TAKEAWAYS

- Simplicity is the key to setup reduction.
- Automate last; eliminate and simplify first.
- Use cheap materials to make mock-ups.

Citations

(All articles taken from the *Lean Manufacturing Advisor*)

Chapter 1: "De-Coupling and Coupling: Keys to Better Cell Design." July 2004: Volume 6, Number 1.

Chapter 2: "Cell Staffing Options (by Vulcan Electric)." March 2001: Volume 2, Number 10.

Chapter 3: "Job Shop Breaks Traditional Rules with 1-Piece Flow Cells." December 2000: Volume 2, Number 7.

Chapter 4: "Cells on Wheels Give Company Ability to Shift Course Quickly." December 2004: Volume 6, Number 7.

Chapter 5: "Time to Take A Radical Step Forward." August 2002: Volume 4, Number 3.

Chapter 6: "Equipment Designed Through 3P Makes a Small Startup Viable." March 2004: Volume 5, Number 10.

Chapter 7: "Takt Time Can Configure a Cell." May 2004: Volume 5, Number 12.

Chapter 8: "You May Need Two Takt Times." February 2003: Volume 4, Number 9.

Chapter 9: "Reducing Scrap Paves the Way For a Big Boost in Capacity." February 2005: Volume 6, Number 9.

Chapter 10: "Building out of Sequence Is Expensive." June 2003: Volume 5, Number 1.

Chapter 11: "Ford Sees Its Future in Flexibility." October 2004: Volume 6, Number 5.

Chapter 12: "Building a Better Body Shop." May 2005: Volume 6, Number 12.

Chapter 13: "Heijunka Can Help Eliminate Production Peaks and Valleys ." October 2002: Volume 4, Number 5.

Chapter 14: "Work Speeds up as Operators Move." December 2003: Volume 5, Number 7.

Chapter 15: "Times, Not Products, Set Schedule." December 2004: Volume 6, Number 7.

Chapter 16: "12-Hour Shifts Help Tire Plant Achieve Its Lean Objectives." November 2003: Volume 5, Number 6.

Chapter 17: "What is in Your Changeover? Probably More Than You Need." October 2004: Volume 6, Number 5.

Chapter 18: "SMED Doubles Parts Output for Metal Stamping Company." October 2003 (online): Volume 5, Number 5.

Chapter 19: "Calculating Changeover Costs Reveals Potential for Savings." August 2005: Volume 7, Number 3.

Chapter 20: "Sequencing Products Leads to Least Changeover Time." August 2003: Volume 5, Number 3.

Chapter 21: "Success with Cardboard & Duct Tape." June 2004: Volume 6, Number 1.

Index